Intelligent companions

INTRODUCTION

The Kennel Club is the United Kingdom's largest organization dedicated to protecting and promoting the health and welfare of all dogs. The Kennel Club divides more than 200 registered breeds in one of seven groups – Gundog, Hound, Pastoral, Terrier, Toy, Utility and Working. Recognized breeds are able to participate in dog events each year. Major events include Crufts (the world's largest dog show), the International **Agility** Festival and Discover Dogs.

The judges at these shows assess a dog's qualities based on the breed's official **purebred** standard. The main considerations are overall appearance, **temperament** and structure. The highest award a dog can win is Best in Show.

Get ready to be introduced to each of the seven groups and learn all about the breeds in each group. Discover each breed's size and appearance, personality, breed history, training recommendations and care tips. You'll be equipped with everything you need to know to become a successful dog owner and family member to your new pup!

Some words are bolded, **like this**. You can find out what they mean on pages 204–205.

Well-rounded companions

The Kennel Club's Gundog group is made up of 37 dog breeds. Dogs in the Gundog group are naturally active and alert. Each breed in this group was developed to work as a hunting dog. They accomplish this task in different ways, however. **Setters** and **pointers** help hunters by locating prey, such as birds. Spaniels chase the birds, forcing them into the air where hunters can see them. Retrievers help their owners by carrying the fallen birds to the hunter once the hunt is complete.

Gundogs are popular pets, especially with active families. Whether these dogs hunt with their owners or hunt alone, they enjoy outdoor activities. Some are impressively fast runners. Others are known for their speed in the water. Some can both run fast and swim well.

Gundog group members that live as companion animals need regular exercise. Many enjoy feeling that they have a purpose. These breeds often excel at organised activities and dog sports, such as agility or **rally** training. Although these dogs share common traits, each one has something unique to offer. Get ready for a close look at each breed!

FUN FACT

The Kennel Club was founded in 1873. The club is the largest dog registration database in the United Kingdom.

Brittany

FUN FACT

A Brittany can smell a group of birds from 69 metres (226 feet) away!

Appearance:
Height: 48 to 51 centimetres (19 to 20 inches)
Weight: 14 to 18 kilograms (30 to 40 pounds)

The Brittany has a short, feathered coat. Most dogs of this breed are orange and white or liver and white. Liver is dark red-brown. Some dogs have patches of colour. Others have roan coats, which means they have light-coloured hairs mixed throughout their coats.

Personality: Brittanys love people, especially children. This bird-dog has a strong hunting **instinct**. The Brittany is a poor match for a home with parakeets or other birds for this reason.

Breed Background: In some countries this dog is called the Brittany Spaniel. While the Brittany looks like a spaniel, he hunts like a pointer.

Country of Origin: France

Training Notes: This smart breed loves pleasing its owner, so training a Brittany can be easy. These dogs respond well to positive and encouraging training methods. Brittanys also excel at competing in dog shows, agility events and hunting tests.

Care Notes: This active breed needs a lot of exercise. Brittanys do well in homes with a large, fenced garden. These short-coated dogs require weekly brushing.

English Setter

FUN FACT

Setters are named for the crouched pose – or set – they take on when hunting game.

Appearance:
Height: 61 to 69 centimetres (24 to 27 inches)
Weight: 20 to 36 kilograms (45 to 80 pounds)

The English Setter has a long, flowing coat. Its coat comes in several colours, such as blue, lemon and orange. Its speckled appearance is often referred to as belton, meaning "blended" or "flecked".

Personality: This playful breed can act downright goofy. English Setters make excellent pets for families with older children. They tend to shy away from younger children who play too roughly, however.

Country of Origin: England

Training Notes: This breed can be stubborn during training. **Persistence** pays off with this smart breed. Basic **obedience** training should begin at a young age with English Setters.

Care Notes: These dogs have a lot of energy. They require daily exercise, such as running in a fenced area. The English Setter's long, feathered coat must be brushed every other day to keep it looking its best.

German Shorthaired Pointer

FUN FACT

A German Shorthaired Pointer's nose is always the same colour as its coat.

Appearance:

Height: 53 to 64 centimetres (21 to 25 inches)
Weight: 20 to 32 kilograms (45 to 70 pounds)

The German Shorthaired Pointer is a versatile all-purpose gundog. The Pointer is named for the pointing position it assumes when hunting. With its eyes looking straight ahead, it raises its tail and one paw. Many people say a pointer looks like an arrow in this pose.

The Pointer has a short, flat coat that resists water. This dog comes in several colours. Liver is among the most common.

Personality: This smart and loyal dog is an excellent pet for active families. Some people say German Shorthaired Pointers are excellent watchdogs too.

Breed Background:

German Shorthaired Pointers stem from dogs known collectively as bird dogs. Some think these dogs **descended** from various German hunting, trail and **track** dogs, such as the Old Spanish Pointer and the Foxhound. The German Shorthaired Pointer's many talents include obedience, retrieving, tracking trials, field trials and hunting tests.

Country of Origin: Germany

Training Notes: A German Shorthaired Pointer is highly trainable. This breed's high energy can be an advantage for training. These active animals enjoy learning new things. Consistency and repetition are key for good training results. This dog does not respond well to harsh discipline. The German Shorthaired Pointer needs an owner with natural authority who provides firm, but calm and consistent training with rules.

Care Notes: German Shorthaired Pointers are incredibly athletic and need a lot of exercise. Their love of the water makes them ideal competitors in dock jumping. This popular canine sport involves chasing a ball that is thrown into the water.

The smooth coat of the German Shorthaired Pointer is easy to groom. Occasional brushing and bathing is all that is required.

FUN FACT

The German Shorthaired Pointer was the first of the Hunt, Point and **Retrieve** breeds to arrive in the UK.

Gordon Setter

FUN FACT

The Gordon Setter is the largest of all setter breeds.

Appearance:

Height: 62 to 66 centimetres (24 to 26 inches)
Weight: 26 to 30 kilograms (56 to 65 pounds)

The Gordon Setter has a black and tan coat with a long, feathered tail. The silky hair may be straight or slightly wavy. Dog enthusiasts are especially fond of this breed's tan eyebrows.

Personality: Gordon Setters are playful puppies. They keep this trait throughout adulthood. They make excellent pets for people who can give them plenty of space. This is not a good breed for city living.

Breed Background: The Gordon Setter got its name from Duke Alexander Gordon, who owned members of the breed. Before this time, the dog was known as the Black and Tan Setter.

Country of Origin: Scotland

Training Notes: Gordon Setters are highly intelligent, so training these dogs can be easy. Positive methods of training are necessary for this breed. Gordon Setters also have incredible memories. Gordon Setters used for hunting can remember places where they found birds for up to one year.

Care Notes: Gordon Setters need daily exercise on a lead or in a fenced area. Weekly bathing and brushing is recommended to keep its coat shiny.

Hungarian Vizsla

Appearance:

Height: 53 to 64 centimetres (21 to 25 inches)
Weight: 20 to 30 kilograms (44 to 66 pounds)

The short-coated Vizsla (*VEESH-lah*) is a russet gold colour. Its hair, eyes, nose and nails are all this colour too. Its coat may feel greasy to the touch.

Personality: A Vizsla's two favourite things are attention and exercise. Owners who give this breed plenty of both get a wonderful companion in return. After a good play session, most Vizslas can be found relaxing at their owners' feet.

Country of Origin: Hungary

Training Notes: Vizslas are smart yet **quirky** dogs. Vizslas are designed to hunt, but owners must be persistent when training this breed. Positive techniques, such as praise and food rewards, work best with Vizslas.

Care Notes: Vizslas need about two hours of intense activity every day. These dogs must run to burn up all their energy. Vizslas also love to swim. Their short coats should be bathed and brushed weekly.

FUN FACT

The Vizsla makes a great pet for owners with sensitive noses. This clean breed has virtually no odour at all.

Irish Setter

FUN FACT

Irish Setters weren't always red. The first members of this breed were mostly white with a few red patches. Dogs with this colouring are now known as Irish Red and White Setters.

Appearance:
Height: 64 to 69 centimetres (25 to 27 inches)
Weight: 27 to 32 kilograms (60 to 70 pounds)

The Irish Setter is known for its soft, deep-red coat. The hair on its head and feet is short. He has longer hair on its ears and the rest of its body.

Personality: This affectionate breed is active and playful. His friendly, affectionate nature makes it a good household dog ready for all the fun and frolic a family will hand it. Irish Setters also tend to bark often.

Country of Origin: Unknown; believed to be Ireland

Training Notes: Irish Setters are smart dogs with a strong hunting instinct. Once these dogs are trained to hunt birds, they never forget the skill. Short, positive training sessions work best for Irish Setters because their lively personality keeps them constantly on the go.

Care Notes: Irish Setters need an active family. These athletic dogs need room to run, such as in a fenced area, or they need to be taken on long walks daily. Grooming an Irish Setter requires regular brushing to prevent its hair from tangling.

Italian Spinone

Appearance:
Height: 58 to 70 centimetres (23 to 28 inches)
Weight: 29 to 39 kilograms (64 to 86 pounds)

The Italian Spinone is best known for the shaggy fur all over its face. This dog has hairy eyebrows as well as a long beard and moustache. The Spinone may be orange and white, brown and white or all white.

FUN FACT

The Italian Spinone is one of the calmest retriever breeds.

Personality: This active breed loves spending time with people. Owners who take these dogs along for hikes will return home with happy pets. Friendly and good-natured, most Italian Spinoni are not **aggressive**.

Country of Origin: Italy

Training Notes: This smart dog is easy to train. Some members of the breed can be stubborn. Spinoni owners should begin **socializing** this breed early.

Care Notes: Owners may want to keep a towel handy with this breed. Many people refer to this dog's slobber as "Spinone slime". These dogs also love to be active, so daily exercise is important. Their medium-length hair should be combed every other week.

FUN FACT

The Korthals Griffon's nickname is the "Supreme Gundog" because of its hunting ability.

Korthals Griffon

Appearance:

Height: 50 to 60 centimetres (20 to 24 inches)
Weight: 23 to 27 kilograms (50 to 60 pounds)

The Korthals Griffon has a thick double coat. The medium-length hair comes in a variety of colours. Brown and grey dogs are the most popular members of this rare breed.

Personality: Korthals Griffons enjoy entertaining their families. These fun-loving dogs thrive when participating in outdoor sports and activities.

Breed Background: This breed was developed by crossing a German Griffon with a French Pointer. Today's Griffons also have retrievers, setters and spaniels in their ancestry.

Country of Origin: Netherlands

Training Notes: This breed is intelligent and easy to train. Griffons are fast learners and want to please their owners.

Care Notes: Korthals Griffon owners should know that this breed loves the water. Whenever this dog is near a pool or lake, it will likely jump in. This highly active breed needs a lot of exercise. Regular brushing will keep a Griffon's wiry coat looking neat.

Pointer

FUN FACT

The Westminster Kennel Club's logo features a Pointer called Sensation.

Appearance:

Height: 61 to 69 centimetres (24 to 27 inches)
Weight: 20 to 34 kilograms (45 to 75 pounds)

A Pointer's muscular body is covered with short hair. Its coat comes in a variety of colours and markings. Among the most common is white with black, lemon or orange markings.

Personality: Pointers are loyal dogs that make great family pets. This breed always wants to be part of the fun. If its human family is outdoors, a Pointer wants to be outside as well.

Breed Background: The oldest of all sporting dogs, Pointers have been working alongside hunters since the 1600s.

Country of Origin: England

Training Notes: Pointers are challenging to train. Owners who make ongoing training a part of their routine usually have the best results with Pointers. Early socialization and basic obedience training will help with this breed's high energy level too.

Care Notes: Like many other sporting breeds, Pointers are active dogs. The ideal owner has a fenced garden or takes this dog for long walks on a daily basis. Pointers require occasional bathing and brushing.

Retriever (Chesapeake Bay)

FUN FACT

The Chesapeake Bay Retriever is the state dog of Maryland, USA.

FAMOUS DOGS

The original Chessies sparking the Chesapeake breed were "Sailor" and "Canton," Newfoundlands rescued from a wrecked English ship off the coast of Maryland, USA.

Appearance:

Height: 53 to 66 centimetres (21 to 26 inches)
Weight: 55 to 80 pounds (25 to 36 kg)

The Chesapeake Bay Retriever has a double coat. The oily outer layer repels water. Even after a bath or swim, this breed can dry itself off just by shaking. Called Chessies, many are brown. The breed also comes in a red colour, called sedge, and a tan colour, called dead grass.

Personality: Chessies are loyal to their human family members. This breed takes time to warm up to strangers and other animals, however.

Country of Origin: United States

Training Notes: Consistent training is a must for this breed. If left untrained these dogs can become bossy with their owners. Early socialization with other animals and with people is important for Chessies.

Care Notes: Chessies need a great deal of exercise. These athletic dogs prefer swimming and games of fetch as opposed to going for walks. Although this breed's coat is short, an owner must brush a Chessie's coat weekly to keep it looking its best.

Retriever (Curly Coated)

Appearance:

Height: 58 to 69 centimetres (23 to 27 inches)
Weight: 29 to 45 kilograms (65 to 100 pounds)

The Curly Coated Retriever has dense curls that can be either black or liver. The curls on the dog's floppy ears are usually looser than the ones on its body. Its coat is waterproof, and even after a swim, it shakes itself a few times and its coat is practically dry.

Personality: Curly Coated Retrievers can seem shy at first. They love their human family members and want to please them. They take time to warm up to new people, however.

Country of Origin:

United Kingdom

Training Notes: This smart breed needs ongoing training because it tends to get bored easily. Slow to mature, the Curly Coated Retriever often acts like a puppy for several years. It's a good idea to get this dog socialized straight away too.

Care Notes: A Curly Coated Retriever needs about an hour of exercise each day. Owners should make sure this time is filled with fun activities. These intelligent dogs are especially good at swimming. This breed needs to be brushed and bathed occasionally.

FUN FACT

Curly Coated Retrievers have a remarkable quality of remembering locations. They are brilliant at retrieving wounded ducks hiding in water or rushes.

Retriever (Flat Coated)

FUN FACT

The breed type was established by Mr Sewallis Evelyn Shirley, the founder of the Kennel Club.

Appearance:

Height: 56 to 61 centimetres (22 to 24 inches)
Weight: 25 to 32 kilograms (55 to 70 pounds)

Many people mistake the Flat Coated Retriever for a mixed breed. But this dog is a purebred. Its dark, flat coat gives the breed its name. Its coat can be either black or liver.

Personality: Flat Coated Retrievers are friendly dogs that make great pets. People looking for a guard dog won't find it here. Sometimes called Flatties, these dogs just want to have fun. The breed's nickname is the "Peter Pan" of dogs.

Breed Background: The Flat Coated Retriever's ancestors include the Newfoundland and the Labrador Retriever.

Country of Origin: United Kingdom

Training Notes: These playful dogs can take more time to train than other breeds. They also take longer to mature. Flat Coated Retrievers need both physical and mental **stimulation**.

Care Notes: Flat Coated Retrievers need a lot of exercise. If owners do not provide an outlet for all its energy, this dog is likely to develop some behaviour problems. Regular brushing and bathing are needed to keep this breed looking its best.

Retriever (Golden)

Appearance:
Height: 53 to 61 centimetres (21 to 24 inches)
Weight: 25 to 34 kilograms (55 to 75 pounds)

The Golden Retriever is one of the most popular gundog breeds. Named for its colour, this dog has a double coat that ranges from light to dark gold. Its coat can be wavy or straight.

Personality: These friendly dogs are known for their obedience and devotion. Golden Retrievers want nothing more than to please their owners.

Country of Origin:
United Kingdom

Training Notes: This intelligent breed is among the easiest dogs to train. Basic obedience training may also strengthen the bond between a Golden Retriever and its human family members. Some Golden Retrievers are trained to work as drug and explosive detecting dogs.

Care Notes: Providing this breed with daily exercise is important in order to maintain physical and mental fitness. A Golden Retriever's water-repellent double coat needs regular brushing and bathing.

FUN FACT

A Golden Retriever always has a lighter coat as a puppy. The colour of a pup's ears is the best sign of what its adult colour will be.

FAMOUS DOGS

The canine stars of the *Air Bud* films are Golden Retrievers.

Retriever (Labrador)

FUN FACT

Labrador Retrievers have been known to jump distances up to 8 metres (27 feet) when retrieving from water.

FAMOUS DOGS

The title character from the *Marley & Me* books and film is a Lab.

Appearance:
Height: 53 to 61 centimetres (21 to 24 inches)
Weight: 25 to 36 kilograms (55 to 80 pounds)

The Labrador Retriever comes in three colours: black, chocolate and yellow. The layered coat is slightly oily. It helps keep the animal warm and afloat when retrieving game in the water. The coat also resists water, so it dries quickly.

Personality: This popular pet is among the friendliest dog breeds. Labs love people of all ages. They make great pets for active families who enjoy the outdoors.

Breed Background: The Labrador Retriever was developed in Newfoundland. This breed was named after the nearby Labrador Sea.

Country of Origin: Canada

Training Notes: These smart animals can be trained for a variety of sports and other tasks. Labs are often the top dogs in obedience competitions. They are also trained to work as drug and arms detection dogs and as guide dogs for blind people. Positive obedience training is essential for Labs.

Care Notes: This active breed needs a lot of exercise. Labs love to run and swim. A Lab's coat must be brushed and bathed occasionally to keep it looking its best.

Retriever (Nova Scotia Duck Tolling)

FUN FACT

The Nova Scotia Duck Tolling Retriever was first known as the "Little River Duck Dog".

Appearance:

Height: 45 to 51 centimetres (18 to 20 inches)
Weight: 16 to 23 kilograms (35 to 50 pounds)

The Nova Scotia Duck Tolling Retriever is a red-orange dog with white on its face, chest and feet. Many dog enthusiasts say the red colour makes this dog look like a fox.

Personality: The smallest of retriever breeds, Nova Scotia Duck Tolling Retrievers are pleasant and happy dogs. This dog can become too independent without a purpose, though. Tollers do best with hunters or active families.

Breed Background: This retriever was named for its hunting style. The dog lures ducks to the hunter, going back and forth between **baiting** and hiding.

Country of Origin: Canada

Training Notes: This breed learns quickly and easily. Owners must make training fun. If a Toller becomes bored, he may develop stubbornness. Calm and positive training methods work best for these dogs. These dogs often enjoy agility or flyball activities.

Care Notes: A Nova Scotia Duck Tolling Retriever needs about an hour of exercise each day. As long as he gets its workout, a Toller can live in either the city or the country. Regular grooming and brushing, such as weekly or every other week, are necessary for this dog's medium-length coat.

Spaniel (American Cocker)

FUN FACT

The American Cocker Spaniel is the smallest member of the gundog group.

FAMOUS DOGS

Lady from the Disney film *Lady and the Tramp* is an American Cocker Spaniel.

Appearance:
Height: 36 to 38 centimetres (14 to 15 inches)
Weight: 9 to 16 kilograms (20 to 35 pounds)

When many people think of American Cocker Spaniels, they imagine dogs with light tan or blond coats. But this sporty breed comes in many other colours, including black, brown and liver. Some American Cocker Spaniels are even particoloured. This means they are a mixture of two or more colours.

Personality: This loyal, loving breed is filled with enthusiasm. When an American Cocker Spaniel greets its favourite people, the dog doesn't just wag its tail. He usually wags its whole backside.

Country of Origin: United States

Training Notes: This intelligent breed is easily trained. Many Cocker Spaniels compete in organised activities, such as agility and obedience.

Care Notes: The Cocker Spaniel's long, floppy ears are a trademark of this breed. Those feathered ears and long coats require a great deal of grooming. Without regular brushing, the hair tangles quickly. Cocker Spaniels also need daily exercise, such as a long walk.

Spaniel (Clumber)

Appearance:
Height: 43 to 51 centimetres (17 to 20 inches)
Weight: 25 to 34 kilograms (55 to 75 pounds)

The Clumber Spaniel is the largest spaniel breed. When a Clumber pup is born, its coat is all white. Over time the dog develops either orange or lemon markings. Its thick, fluffy coat remains mostly white even as an adult, however.

Personality: Clumber Spaniels are usually quiet pets. Their personalities can range from friendly to **aloof**. People who want an outgoing dog should spend time with a whole litter. The puppy that greets you first is often the friendliest.

Country of Origin: France

Training Notes: Clumber Spaniels need basic obedience training. These large dogs can be mischievous. Even a trained Clumber Spaniel will steal food from a countertop if the opportunity arises.

Care Notes: Owning this heavy-coated breed means lots of grooming. Clumber Spaniels are known for loud snoring and drooling. Many owners keep towels nearby. Clumber Spaniels also enjoy daily walks with their owners.

FUN FACT

It is believed that the Clumber Spaniel was developed from the Basset Hound and early Alpine Spaniels, influencing the long, low body and heavy head of the Clumber.

Spaniel (Cocker)

FUN FACT

Cocker Spaniels are named after birds called woodcocks. These birds are the most common animals the breeds hunt.

FAMOUS DOGS

Prince William, Duke of Cambridge, and Catherine, Duchess of Cambridge, own a Cocker Spaniel called Lupo.

Appearance:
Height: 38 to 43 centimetres (15 to 17 inches)
Weight: 12 to 15 kilograms (26 to 34 pounds)

Some people say that the Cocker Spaniel has a "melting expression" with soft, dark eyes. Its silky coat can be solid black, red-brown, or various shades of red.

Personality: The Cocker Spaniel shares many traits with its American cousin, the American Cocker Spaniel. Both breeds make pleasant pets. Cocker Spaniels spend more time working as hunting dogs than American Cocker Spaniels do.

Breed Background: Cocker Spaniels were recognised as a separate breed from Field and Springer Spaniels soon after the formation of the Kennel Club in 1873.

Country of Origin: England

Training Notes: This intelligent breed learns quickly. Gentle, positive training works best with Cocker Spaniels. They respond well to praise.

Care Notes: Cocker Spaniels love to play. A couple of sessions of fetch each day are enough of a workout for this breed. These dogs also need to be brushed and **stripped** regularly.

Spaniel (English Springer)

FUN FACT

The Springer Spaniel is the fastest of all the Spaniel breeds.

Appearance:

Height: 48 to 51 centimetres (19 to 20 inches)
Weight: 18 to 23 kilograms (40 to 50 pounds)

English Springer Spaniels have varying coat patterns and hair lengths. Common colours for this breed include black and white, liver and white and red and white. These graceful dogs also have long, lush ears.

Personality: All Springers love to play and spend time with their human family members. These dogs are known for their affectionate personalities. English Springer Spaniels also have a lot of energy and a big hunting drive.

Breed Background: Springer Spaniels were bred to act like several hunting dogs in one. They can point and retrieve game. He took its present name in 1900 after being known for many years as the Norfolk Spaniel.

Country of Origin: England

Training Notes: Some English Springer Spaniels have a natural hunting ability. Still, these dogs must be trained to perform this activity. Without positive training, Springers can become obnoxious and pushy.

Care Notes: To prevent **mats**, Springers should be brushed weekly. This breed needs regular exercise and loves to swim and play fetch.

FUN FACT

The Sussex Spaniel was named after Sussex, England, where the breed was developed.

Spaniel (Sussex)

Appearance:
Height: 33 to 38 centimetres (13 to 15 inches)
Weight: 16 to 20 kilograms (35 to 45 pounds)

With its long body and short legs, the Sussex Spaniel looks like a small Cocker Spaniel. The breed is also known for its golden-liver colour. He has a feathery coat with wavy ears and big, hazel eyes.

Personality: Sussex Spaniels offer owners the best of both worlds when it comes to personality. At home these dogs make calm and well-mannered pets. Outside, however, they transform into much more active animals.

Country of Origin: England

Training Notes: Sussex Spaniels are fast learners. Still, some can take time to obey commands. Owners should be patient when training Sussex Spaniels and always use heartfelt praise.

Care Notes: Owners should take their Sussex Spaniels for long walks or hikes regularly. This breed also appreciates the company of other dogs. Its soft coat should be brushed weekly.

Spaniel (Welsh Springer)

FUN FACT

The history of the Welsh Springer Spaniel begins as far back as 7000 BC.

Appearance:

Height: 43 to 48 centimetres (17 to 19 inches)
Weight: 16 to 25 kilograms (35 to 55 pounds)

The Welsh Springer Spaniel has a red and white feathered coat. The hair is naturally straight and lies flat against the dog's body. Its coat is considered waterproof and **weatherproof**.

Personality: Welsh Springers love their human family members. They love children who treat them respectfully. Welsh Springers can be slow to accept strangers.

Country of Origin: Wales

Training Notes: These dogs train easily, but early socialization is important. Welsh Springer Spaniels that aren't exposed to people as puppies can become shy as adult dogs.

Care Notes: This athletic dog needs daily exercise or walks. Regular brushing is important for Welsh Springer Spaniels. These dogs also need their ears cleaned often. Like other spaniel breeds, Welsh Springer Spaniels are prone to ear infections.

FUN FACT

All Weimaraner puppies are born with blue eyes. Their eyes turn yellow as the dogs get older.

Weimaraner

Appearance:

Height: 58 to 69 centimetres (23 to 27 inches)
Weight: 25 to 39 kilograms (55 to 85 pounds)

Weimaraners are known for their muscular bodies. They are large and athletic. They also have long, floppy ears that hang down the side of their heads.

Weimaraners have a short, smooth coat. These dogs are also known for their unusual colour. Their coats are a unique silvery grey. The breed is nicknamed the "Grey Ghost".

Personality: Weimaraners are happy, loving dogs. They make excellent family pets. However, they tend to bark a lot. Sometimes they do this to announce a visitor. Other times they simply enjoy making a noise. Weimaraners should not be in the same household as small pets, such as rabbits or hamsters. Their hunting instinct is too strong and they may end up hurting the small animals.

Breed Background: The Weimaraner breed was developed in the early 1800s as a hunting dog in Germany. It is descended from the Bloodhound.

Country of Origin: Germany

Training Notes: This breed is intelligent yet independent. Most times a Weimaraner is easy to train. This dog tends to get bored during training, however. Short, focused training sessions work best with a Weimaraner. Puppy obedience classes should begin right away.

Care Notes: Weimaraners are speedy runners and need lots of exercise every day. They should be taken on a long, daily walk or jog. These dogs also love opportunites to run free in a large, fenced area.

This short-haired breed is easy to groom and only needs a bath every few weeks. Its coat should be brushed with a firm-**bristled** brush to help keep it shiny.

FUN FACT

A Weimaraner has many talents. Some of its talents include: tracking, police work, service for the disabled and elderly, search-and-rescue work and agility.

Other gundog breeds

German Wirehaired Pointer ▶

Appearance:
Height: 56 to 67 centimetres (22 to 27 inches)
Weight: 25 to 34 kilograms (55 to 75 pounds)
Known for: ability to hunt in harsh conditions
Country of Origin: Germany

Hungarian Wire Haired Vizsla ▶

Appearance:
Height: 54 to 62 centimetres (22 to 25 inches)
Weight: 20 to 30 kilograms (44 to 66 pounds)
Known for: heavy build and wiry coat
Country of Origin: Hungary

Irish Red and White Setter

Appearance:
Height: 64 to 69 centimetres (25 to 27 inches)
Weight: 27 to 32 kilograms (60 to 70 pounds)
Known for: being the older of the two Irish Setter breeds
Country of Origin: Ireland

Lagotto Romagnolo ▶

Appearance:

Height: 41 to 48 centimetres (16 to 19 inches)

Weight: 11 to 16 kilograms (24 to 35 pounds)

Known for: curly coat

Country of Origin: Italy

Spaniel (American Water)

Appearance:

Height: 38 to 46 centimetres (15 to 18 inches)

Weight: 15 to 21 kilograms (33 to 45 pounds)

Known for: retrieving waterfowl

Country of Origin: United States

Spaniel (Field)

Appearance:

Height: 40 to 46 centimetres (16 to 18 inches)

Weight: 18 to 25 kilograms (40 to 55 pounds)

Known for: dedication as a hunter

Country of Origin: England

Hunting hounds

The Kennel Club's Hound group is made up of 37 dog breeds. Most dogs in the hound group were developed to work as hunting dogs. Scent hounds help hunters by locating prey with their noses. These dogs have a highly developed sense of smell that is even more sensitive than that of other dog breeds. Sighthounds, also called gazehounds, rely on their sharp eyesight and wide range of vision to locate prey.

Hounds vary in their personalities as much as they do in their appearances. Some are too loud to keep in flats or with close-by neighbours. Many hounds bark or howl frequently. Many are extremely athletic, while some are couch potatoes. Some are even both active and lazy – depending on the time of day. Some make excellent pets. Others prefer to spend their time in the field.

Whether they are working dogs or companions, hounds almost always have a desire to hunt. For this reason, fenced gardens and leads are important for keeping them safe. Although these dogs share the urge to hunt, they all have something special to offer dog lovers. Get ready for a close-up look at each hound breed!

FUN FACT

The Kennel Club organises many initiatives to aid dog owners in caring for their dogs. The Kennel Club runs Petlog, which is the UK's largest database for microchipped pets, in order to reunite lost dogs with their owners.

Afghan Hound

FUN FACT

An Afghan Hound can run up to 64 kilometres (40 miles) per hour!

FAMOUS DOGS

Pablo Picasso created a 15-metre (50-foot) sculpture based on one of his Afghan Hounds. The piece stands at Chicago's Daley Plaza in the USA.

Appearance:
Height: 68 to 74 centimetres (27 to 29 inches)
Weight: 23 to 27 kilograms (50 to 60 pounds)

With its large body and long, silky hair, the Afghan Hound is an elegant breed. These dogs have long, narrow heads that help when hunting. They can see things both in front of them and far to each side.

Personality: Afghans are athletic dogs that love their human families. Fenced gardens are a smart idea for this breed because they are sighthounds. An Afghan won't just notice a squirrel – it will chase it down.

Breed Background: One of the oldest dog breeds, the Afghan Hound was developed to hunt gazelle, deer and even leopards.

Countries of Origin: Afghanistan, Iran, Pakistan

Training Notes: While Afghan Hounds are smart, they are also sensitive. They respond well to patience and lots of praise.

Care Notes: Afghans need a lot of exercise. They love to run in a large, contained area or be taken on daily walks. These dogs need their long coats brushed and washed daily.

Basenji

Appearance:

Height: 40 to 43 centimetres (16 to 17 inches)
Weight: 9 to 1 kilograms (20 to 24 pounds)

This short-haired breed has several features that make it easy to recognise. First, people usually notice the dog's tightly curled tail. The breed also has a wrinkled forehead and large, pointed ears.

Personality: The Basenji's voice box is shaped differently than that of other breeds. For this reason Basenjis can't bark like other dogs. Instead they make a crowing-yodelling sound.

Breed Background: The Basenji was and is still used to hunt lions in Africa.

Area of Origin: Congo Basin

Training Notes: These intelligent dogs are extremely independent, so training takes time and effort. Early obedience training is important for Basenjis. Socialization at a young age is also a good idea.

Care Notes: Basenjis are known for getting into trouble when the opportunity arises. Owners who leave their belongings out may find them chewed up. Keeping a Basenji busy with plenty of exercise may help with its chewing habits. These dogs also need occasional bathing and brushing to keep them looking their best.

FUN FACT

Some hounds hunt with their noses. Others rely on their eyes. The Basenji uses both sight and scent in the field.

Basset Fauve De Bretagne

FUN FACT

The Basset Fauve De Bretagne is sometimes called the **Fawn** Brittany Basset.

Appearance:
Height: 32 to 38 centimetres (13 to 15 inches)
Weight: 11 to 16 kilograms (25 to 35 pounds)

The Basset Fauve De Bretagne's reddish coat is wiry in texture. Its legs are slightly shorter than the length of its back, but the Basset Fauve De Bretagne does not sit as low to the ground as the Basset Hound.

Personality: A Basset Fauve De Bretagne is lively, sweet and devoted. It makes a suitable pet for a small home and garden. This dog is also friendly with children.

Breed Background: It is believed that this breed came from crossing a Griffon Fauve De Bretagne, a breed that is now extinct, and a Brittany Basset. The breed worked with flocks of sheep in the fields of France.

Country of Origin: France

Training Notes: The Basset Fauve De Bretagne needs firm and consistent training. It is also known for performing tricks for food!

Care Notes: The Basset Fauve De Bretagne loves to exercise! Because of this dog's short coat, grooming is an easy chore. It should be brushed and bathed occasionally to keep it looking its best.

Basset Hound

Appearance:

Height: 33 to 38 centimetres (13 to 15 inches)
Weight: 20 to 29 kilograms (45 to 65 pounds)

The Basset Hound has a heavy body, short legs and the longest ears of any dog breed. Many people think this breed has a sad expression because of the animal's droopy eyes but nothing could be further from the truth.

Personality: Bassets are affectionate and loyal dogs. They especially love spending time with children. Children must be taught to treat these dogs with respect, however. Playing too rough with this breed can injure its long back.

Breed Background: Basset Hounds were developed by breeding Bloodhounds down to a smaller size.

Countries of Origin: France, United Kingdom

Training Notes: Basset Hounds are stubborn dogs but easy to train. These dogs have a strong urge to hunt prey, especially hares, so training should begin at the puppy stage.

Care Notes: Because Basset Hounds are more likely to become **obese** than other breeds, daily exercise, including walks, is necessary. Weekly grooming, such as brushing the coat, is recommended. Owners must also clean their Basset Hounds' long ears frequently to prevent infection.

FUN FACT

Breeders who developed the Basset Hound chose dogs with white on their tails. The bright tip helped hunters spot the dogs even if they were in high brush.

Bavarian Mountain Hound

FUN FACT

The Bavarian Mountain Hound hails from Bavaria, Germany, where it is known as the *Bayerische Gebirgsschweisshund*.

Appearance:
Height: 44 to 52 centimetres (18 to 21 inches)
Weight: 18 to 25 kilograms (40 to 55 pounds)

The Bavarian Mountain Hound has a short, shiny coat, usually characterised by a darker face, head and ears. Its coat is deer red, tan or fawn with interspersed black hairs. This pattern is called **brindle**.

Personality: There aren't many dogs more loyal than a Bavarian Mountain Hound. It makes a good family dog and is friendly with children. It can be aloof with strangers, however.

Breed Background: The Bavarian Mountain Hound was bred to be a hunting dog in Germany's mountainous regions. He specialises in tracking large wounded game, such as wild boar and deer. The Bavarian Mountain Hound can follow game over huge distances many hours after the game's trail has been left.

Country of Origin: Germany

Training Notes: The Bavarian Mountain Hound is responsive to a respectful owner. He easily learns commands and obedience with positive reinforcement, such as treats or praise.

Care Notes: The Bavarian Mountain Hound needs a considerable amount of exercise each day. Its nose may lead it to trouble or danger, so walking without a lead is not recommended.

Beagle

Appearance:

Height: 33 to 40 centimetres (13 to 16 inches)
Weight: 9 to 11 kilograms (20 to 25 pounds)

Beagles can be almost any colour, except all white. By far the most popular variety is the **tricolour**. This combination is made up of a black **saddle**, tan head and middle and white everywhere else.

Personality: Beagles are one of the most popular hounds, both as a family companion and in the show ring. They are friendly with their owners and most strangers. Beagles have a loud bark, however.

Country of Origin: United Kingdom

Training Notes: Beagles are smart dogs. Non-hunting Beagles must be kept on leads or in fenced gardens, however. These determined animals will follow any scent that tempts them. Because of their independent personality, short training sessions may work best with Beagles.

Care Notes: Beagles are playful and need a fair amount of exercise each day. Despite their short coats, Beagles need frequent baths. If anything smelly is nearby, this breed will surely roll in it. Weekly brushing is also important for these shedders.

FUN FACT

Beagles have a special sound they make when hunting. They use it to let the hunter know they are following the scent of their prey.

FAMOUS DOGS

The famous *Peanuts* cartoon character Snoopy is a Beagle.

Bloodhound

FUN FACT

The Bloodhound was first used in England for law enforcement in the early 1800s. They were used to track thieves and **poachers**.

FAMOUS DOGS

Napoleon in the Disney fild *Aristocats* (1970) is a Bloodhound.

Appearance:
Height: 61 to 66 centimetres (24 to 26 inches)
Weight: 36 to 41 kilograms (80 to 90 pounds)

Bloodhounds have sturdy bodies, long ears and lots of wrinkles. The breed's short, thin coat comes in several colours. Black and tan or red are common coat colours for this dog.

Personality: A Bloodhound can make a wonderful pet. People considering buying this breed should know how much Bloodhounds drool – a lot!

Breed Background: Some people think that the Bloodhound got its name from its ability to smell blood. Bloodhounds have the most powerful noses of any dog breed. They actually got their name from their pure bloodlines.

Countries of Origin: Belgium, England, France, Scotland

Training Notes: Owners can train Bloodhounds to do almost anything – except not follow their noses. Obedience training should begin during the puppy stage for these dogs.

Care Notes: Bloodhounds need lots of daily exercise to prevent boredom. These dogs should be brushed and bathed weekly to help them look and smell their best.

Borzoi

FUN FACT

The Borzoi is also known as the Russian Wolfhound. The word ***borzii*** is Russian for "swift".

Appearance:
Height: 68 to 74 centimetres (27 to 29 inches)
Weight: 27 to 48 kilograms (60 to 105 pounds)

Borzois are large but graceful dogs. Their long, silky coats can be flat, curly or wavy. Any colour is acceptable for this breed.

Personality: The Borzoi is known for its incredible speed and endurance. As active as they are, these dogs love spending time with their owners. Dog enthusiasts say the Borzoi is among the most loving and gentle dog breeds.

Breed Background:
The Borzoi was developed by crossing Arabian Greyhounds with sheepdogs.

Country of Origin: Russia

Training Notes: Borzois need extra time and patience when training. They are naturally stubborn. Using praise and rewards, such as treats, may help a Borzoi warm up to obedience training.

Care Notes: Similar to other sighthounds, the Borzoi cannot be trusted off its lead in public. A high, fenced garden is ideal for daily running and exercise. This breed's long coat should be brushed regularly to keep it shiny and mat-free.

Dachshund

FUN FACT

Some people call Dachshunds hot dogs because of their length. But the food was actually named after the animal. Hot dogs were called "dachshund sausages" when they were first created.

Appearance:

Standard
Height: 20 to 27 centimetres (8 to 11 inches)
Weight: 9 to 12 kilograms (20 to 26 pounds)

Miniature
Height: 13 to 18 centimetres (5 to 7 inches)
Weight: less than 5 kilograms (11 pounds)

Dachshunds are long dogs that stand low to the ground. Their coats can be smooth-haired, wire-haired or long-haired. These dogs come in two sizes – standard or miniature. Both are members of the same breed. The most common Dachshund colours are black and tan, red and silver dapple.

Personality: The Dachshund is a popular pet that bonds closely with its owners. The breed is an excellent house-dog and will guard against any unwelcome guests. Its bark can be surprsingly deep for a small dog.

Breed Background: The Dachshund breed can be traced back to working dogs in Germany.

Country of Origin: Germany

Training Notes: This breed is smart but stubborn. Owners may spend a lot of time training a Dachshund, especially with house-training. Patience and persistence are recommended with this breed. Dachshunds respond well to positive rewards, such as praise or treats.

Care Notes: Dachshunds love to dig. For this reason owners must supervise their pets whenever they spend time outside. To avoid becoming overweight, Dachshunds should exercise regularly. Weekly brushing or combing is important for all coat types of this breed.

FUN FACT

This breed has short legs and sits low to the ground for a good reason. Back in the 1600s in Germany, Dachshunds were used for hunting rabbits and badgers. They follow these animals into their underground nests.

Deerhound

FUN FACT

Deerhounds are so easy-going that they cannot be trained to be watchdogs. Being aggressive just isn't in their nature.

Appearance:
Height: 71 to 76 centimetres (28 to 30 inches)
Weight: 37 to 46 kilograms (80 to 100 pounds)

The Deerhound's coat is thick and shaggy. Most Deerhounds are dark blue-grey, although the breed comes in a variety of other colours too. Some are sandy-red, shades of yellow or red fawn.

Personality: This friendly, athletic dog can make a great family pet as long as it gets its exercise. The only thing a Deerhound enjoys more than going for a long walk is resting afterwards.

Country of Origin: Scotland

Training Notes: This breed can be difficult to train. Deerhounds delight in their owners' praise, but they prefer doing what they like. Early socialization and obedience training may help with this issue.

Care Notes: Exercise is very important for Deerhounds. They need space to run on a daily basis. Deerhounds are shedders. Their coats need brushing about twice per week to remove dead hair.

Finnish Spitz

Appearance:

Height: 39 to 50 centimetres (16 to 20 inches)
Weight: 14 to 16 kilograms (31 to 35 pounds)

The Finnish Spitz looks a bit like a fox. His square body is covered with a thick double coat. Males usually have fuller coats than females. All dogs are a golden-red colour and can range from a pale honey to a deep red-brown.

Personality: Developed as hunting dogs, Finnish Spitzes remain highly active. Many still hunt in their native country. They can also make excellent pets for families because they get along well with children. Intensely loyal, a Finnish Spitz will protect its human family when necessary.

Country of Origin: Finland

Training Notes: The Finnish Spitz is a smart dog but bores easily. To keep this breed focused, train often but only for short periods of time. These dogs respond well to positive praise and rewards.

Care Notes: A Finnish Spitz needs a lot of exercise each day. A rigorous play session in a fenced area can help use up this dog's energy. Because it is a heavy shedder, regular brushing and bathing is important.

FUN FACT

The Finnish Spitz is the national dog of Finland.

Foxhound

FUN FACT

Foxhounds are bred to run for many kilometres at a time.

Appearance:

Height: 58 to 64 centimetres (23 to 25 inches)
Weight: 29 to 32 kilograms (65 to 70 pounds)

The Foxhound is an athletic gundog. It is a courageous and passionate hunter with a high amount of energy.

The Foxhound has a short, tricoloured coat. The hair is black, white and tan and has a rough texture. This hard texture protects the dog from both harsh weather and low branches.

Personality: Foxhounds are friendly, gentle dogs. Despite their loving nature, they're not usually kept as pets. These dogs are meant for people who will take them hunting often. They are happiest when working as part of a pack of Foxhounds in the field.

Breed Background: The Foxhound is one of the few dog breeds that continues to be bred for its original purpose – hunting. It dates back to the 1800s in Great Britain. Foxhounds were developed by crossing a variety of hounds with the Bulldog, Greyhound and Fox Terrier.

Country of Origin: United Kingdom

Training Notes: As pack animals, these dogs learn many hunting techniques from watching their fellow Foxhounds. Training Foxhounds requires patience and understanding. They respond well to loving but firm leadership. They may not be as responsive as some breeds, so training requires patience.

Care Notes: Daily exercise is ideal for this breed. Foxhounds are typically extremely active, so this breed will get along very well with an active family. Foxhounds enjoy a daily, long walk or jog. Do not take a Foxhound off its lead unless you are in a safe, fenced area. It likes to follow its nose!

A Foxhound's short coat is easy to care for. It should be brushed regularly to keep its coat looking shiny.

FUN FACT

There are two types of Foxhounds: field lines and show lines.

Greyhound

Appearance:
Height: 69 to 76 centimetres (27 to 30 inches)
Weight: 27 to 36 kilograms (60 to 80 pounds)

The Greyhound looks like it was built for speed. Its thin body and long legs make it the fastest dog in the Kennel Club. This sighthound also has a long, thin head that gives it a wide field of vision. It can see what is behind it without turning its head.

Personality: Greyhounds make ideal pets for active families. Despite their large size, these loving animals think they are lapdogs. Greyhounds are highly affectionate, faithful and gentle.

Country of Origin: Unknown; believed to be Egypt

Training Notes: Greyhounds are easy to train but require patience. Early obedience training works well with Greyhounds.

Care Notes: Because of their tendency to run, Greyhounds need daily exercise in a large, fenced area. Their short coats do not require much grooming except occasional brushing and bathing.

FUN FACT

Greyhounds can reach speeds over 70 kilometres (45 miles) per hour after running just 15 metres (50 feet)!

FAMOUS DOGS

Harry Potter author J.K. Rowling adopted her Greyhound, Sapphire, from an animal shelter.

Ibizan Hound

FUN FACT

The Ibizan Hound's nickname is the "Beezer".

Appearance:
Height: 56 to 74 centimetres (22 to 29 inches)
Weight: 19 to 25 kilograms (42 to 55 pounds)

The Ibizan Hound has two coat types: short-haired or wire-haired. The breed also comes in three colours, including chestnut or lion solid colour, white or a combination of these. The dog's flesh-coloured nose and eye rims give the breed a unique look.

Personality: Ibizan Hounds are affectionate and highly loyal to their human family members. These dogs take more time to warm up to strangers, however.

Country of Origin: Egypt

Training Notes: This breed learns quickly but becomes bored easily. Owners will have the best luck keeping training sessions short and fun. Early socialization training may also help Ibizan Hounds with warming up to new people.

Care Notes: Fenced gardens give Ibizan Hounds the space to move that this breed needs. It is important that the fence is at least 1.8 metres (6 feet) high. An Ibizan Hound can jump anything shorter. Its rough, short coat requires only occasional brushing and bathing.

Irish Wolfhound

FUN FACT

An Irish Wolfhound can measure up to 2 metres (7 feet) tall when standing on its hind legs.

Appearance:

Height: 71 to 79 centimetres (28 to 31 inches)
Weight: 41 to 55 kilograms (90 to 120 pounds)

Everything about the Irish Wolfhound is large. But one of its greatest attributes is its perfection of balance. The Irish Wolfhound is the tallest of all dog breeds. Many people joke that this dog looks more like a horse than a dog. Horses definitely do not have this breed's rough and wiry coat, however.

After its size, the breed is best known for its shaggy coat. Its coat can be smooth or rough.

Personality: Irish Wolfhounds are kind and sweet-tempered. Willing to please, they are unconditionally loyal to their owners. They are also great with children, but it should be supervised around small children because of their size.

Breed Background: The Irish Wolfhound is one of the oldest breeds still living today. It dates back to AD 391. The breed was developed to hunt elk, wild boars and wolves.

Country of Origin: Ireland

Training Notes: It is essential to begin training this breed while it is a puppy. Handling an **unruly** adult Irish Wolfhound is a challenging task for most people. If properly trained, Irish Wolfhounds will excel at dog sports in the show ring.

Care Notes: New owners of this breed should be prepared to buy lots of dog food. An adult Irish Wolfhound can eat 11 kilograms (25 pounds) of food in just one week. Despite its size, an Irish Wolfhound doesn't need much exercise. Weekly brushing is important for these shaggy dogs.

FUN FACT

The Irish Wolfhound breed nearly died out during the Great Famine of the 1840s in Ireland. The breed has been brought back and is now very popular.

Otterhound

FUN FACT

The Otterhound is considered one of the most endangered dog breeds worldwide. It is rarer than the Giant Panda.

Appearance:
Height: 61 to 69 centimetres (24 to 27 inches)
Weight: 30 to 52 kilograms (66 to 115 pounds)

The Otterhound's coat is dense and harsh, and its hair always looks messy. The thick double coat comes in many different colours and combinations. The most common combination is black and tan.

Personality: Otterhounds are loving pets. They are best suited for active families. Owners should take this dog along when going to the beach or lake whenever possible. Otterhounds greatly enjoy swimming and being in the water.

Countries of Origin: United Kingdom, France

Training Notes: Otterhound owners should make early socialization a top priority. Training may require patience, persistence and positive rewards and praise.

Care Notes: This breed needs plenty of space for regular exercise. Weekly brushing is important to keep an Otterhound's hair clean and tangle-free.

Pharaoh Hound

FUN FACT

The Pharoah Hound is the National Dog of Malta.

Appearance:

Height: 53 to 63 centimetres (21 to 25 inches)
Weight: 20 to 25 kilograms (45 to 55 pounds)

The Pharaoh Hound's short coat, muscular body and pointed ears make this breed easy to spot anywhere. Its coat can be tan or rich tan with white markings on its chest, face, tail and toes.

Personality: Pharaoh Hounds love their human family members and are entertaining. These dogs aren't as friendly with new people, however. When a stranger arrives, a Pharaoh Hound can become aloof.

Breed Background: The Pharaoh Hound looks a lot like dogs in Ancient Egyptian art. This is no accident, as the breed dates back to 1,000 BC in this part of the world.

Country of Origin: Egypt

Training Notes: Pharaoh Hounds are highly intelligent and enjoy pleasing their owners. The breed can be stubborn, so training is important early on.

Care Notes: This breed feels cold easily. Dogs living in cooler climates should wear coats for time spent outdoors. These athletic dogs also need daily exercise. Their short coats need to be brushed every other week.

Rhodesian Ridgeback

FUN FACT

A Rhodesian Ridgeback can keep pace with a running horse for up to 48 kilometres (30 miles).

Appearance:
Height: 61 to 69 centimetres (24 to 27 inches)
Weight: 29 to 41 kilograms (65 to 90 pounds)

The Rhodesian Ridgeback is a large, muscular dog with a short coat. The breed is easy to identify by the ridge on its back. This long line is created by fur that grows in the opposite direction from the other hair in this area. The breed was named for this unusual feature.

Personality: Rhodesian Ridgebacks make ideal companions for families with older children. Their high activity level makes them a perfect match for active people. This is a dog that wants to spend lots of time outdoors.

Breed Background: Also known as the African Lion Dog, this breed was developed to hunt large cats.

Area of Origin: Rhodesia (present-day Zimbabwe), southern Africa

Training Notes: This smart breed is highly independent. Patient and consistent training works best with Rhodesians.

Care Notes: Rhodesian Ridgebacks are very athletic and need at least an hour of exercise each day. Because they have short coats, Rhodesians shed very little and require only weekly brushing.

FUN FACT

The Rhodesian Ridgeback dates back to the 1500s.

Saluki

FUN FACT

The name Saluki is believed to have originated from the long-gone Arabian city of Saluk or from the town of Seleukia in ancient Syria.

Appearance:

Height: 58 to 71 centimetres (23 to 28 inches)
Weight: 14 to 25 kilograms (31 to 55 pounds)

The Saluki looks a lot like a long-haired Greyhound. He has a long, thin body that helps it move quickly. These dogs are lean but incredibly muscular. Their feathery coats come in a variety of colours, including white, cream, red, tricolour or black and tan.

Personality: Salukis can be shy and take their time warming up to people. These dogs are suited for active families who will take the time to challenge them both physically and mentally.

Breed Background: Royal Ancient Egyptians turned their Salukis into mummies when the dogs died.

Country of Origin: Egypt

Training Notes: The Saluki can be naughty if left alone. The Saluki's aloof nature can make training difficult. Patience and consistency are important, as well as early obedience training.

Care Notes: One of the best ways to provide this breed with the exercise it needs is to take it jogging. Salukis can keep up with even the most athletic human runners. These dogs don't shed a lot, but they should still be brushed weekly and bathed occasionally.

Whippet

FUN FACT

In the north-east of England, some racing Whippets have been known to cover over 180 metres (591 feet) in as little as 12 seconds!

Appearance:
Height: 44 to 51 centimetres (18 to 20 inches)
Weight: 9 to 18 kilograms (20 to 40 pounds)

Whippets are medium-sized sighthounds with great speed and balance. These short-haired dogs come in a variety of colours and markings, including black, blue, cream, red and white. Whippets are a breed of muscularity and neatness paired with power and elegance.

Personality: Named for their whip-like speed, these dogs are surprisingly calm when they're not playing. They enjoy napping on the floor or sofa. Some dogs will even snuggle with their favourite human family member.

Country of Origin: England

Training Notes: Whippets are smart but sensitive. They need positive, gentle training. They respond well to praise and other rewards.

Care Notes: These athletic dogs excel at canine sports, such as agility. Without an organised activity, Whippets need a large amount of daily exercise. Their short coats should also be brushed weekly and bathed occasionally.

Other hound breeds

Basset Griffon Vendeen (Petit) ▶

Appearance:
Height: 34 to 38 centimetres (14 to 15 inches)
Weight: 11 to 16 kilograms (25 to 35 pounds)
Known for: its nickname – the PBGV
Country of Origin: France

Cirneco Dell'Etna ▼

Appearance:
Height: 42 to 52 centimetres (17 to 20 inches)
Weight: 10 to 12 kilograms (22 to 26 pounds)
Known for: ability to hunt by sight and sound
Country of Origin: Italy

Harrier ▶

Appearance:
Height: 48 to 50 centimetres (19 to 21 inches)
Weight: 18 to 27 kilograms (40 to 60 pounds)
Known for: being talented hunters and friendly pets
Country of Origin: United Kingdom

Norwegian Elkhound

Appearance:
Height: 49 to 52 centimetres (20 to 21 inches)
Weight: 20 to 23 kilograms (44 to 51 pounds)
Known for: loud voice
Country of Origin: Norway

Portuguese Podengo

Appearance:
Height: 20 to 30 centimetres (8 to 12 inches)
Weight: 4 to 5 kilograms (9 to 11 pounds)
Known for: National Breed of Portugal
Country of Origin: Portugal

Herding dogs

The Kennel Club's Pastoral group is made up of 37 dog breeds. Pastoral dogs are skilled and hard-working. These dogs were first developed to drive animals such as sheep, reindeer and cattle. The dogs worked with farmers to move large flocks or herds from one area to another. They would run frantically, bark aggressively and nip at the animals' heels to move them forward.

Many pastoral dogs have also become popular as pets. These smart dogs enjoy being useful. Whether they are competing in an organised activity or learning commands in their own back garden, they take their jobs seriously. Many breeds have a strong desire to please their owners.

Because of their high energy levels, pastoral dogs aren't for everyone. They can be loud and **boisterous**. Some will even try to herd small children if they have nothing else to do. Owners must provide these dogs with plenty of activity.

Pastoral dogs come in a wide range of sizes and coat types. From the small Corgi to the giant Old English Sheepdog, pastoral dog-lovers are bound to find a breed that is right for them.

FUN FACT

Each year the Kennel Club registers around 250,000 dogs, across 212 breeds.

Australian Cattle Dog

FUN FACT

The Australian Cattle Dog is also known as the Australian Heeler.

Appearance:

Height: 43 to 51 centimetres (17 to 20 inches)
Weight: 14 to 20 kilograms (30 to 45 pounds)

Australian Cattle Dogs have a short double coat. It comes in either blue, blue speckle or red speckle. Some dogs have dark fur around one or both eyes. This marking makes it look like the dog is wearing a mask.

Personality: Australian Cattle Dogs make loving and loyal pets. They can be wary of strangers though. When they work as cattle herders, Australian Cattle Dogs are determined and courageous.

Breed Background: The breed was developed by carefully crossing the Dingo, the Kelpie, the Dalmatian and the Bull Terrier.

Country of Origin: Australia

Training Notes: Australian Cattle Dogs are smart and highly trainable. They respond especially well to rewards. Some owners train Australian Cattle Dogs for performance events, such as herding or agility competitions.

Care Notes: Australian Cattle Dogs can make great pets for the right people. Owners should be prepared to provide plenty of activity though. The breed needs two to three hours of exercise each day.

Australian Shepherd

Appearance:
Height: 46 to 58 centimetres (18 to 23 inches)
Weight: 18 to 29 kilograms (40 to 65 pounds)

The Australian Shepherd has medium-length fur. Many Australian Shepherds are merles, which means that the coat has a mixture of dark patches and lighter markings.

Personality: Australian Shepherds have strong personalities. Bred to herd sheep, they can be pushy pets. Some have even been known to try to herd children.

Country of Origin:
United States

Training Notes:
Australian Shepherds are highly intelligent and eager to please their owners. Positive training methods, such as treats and lots of praise, work best with this breed.

Care Notes: Although the Australian Shepherd's coat is medium-length, this breed doesn't need a lot of grooming. Regular brushing and occasional baths are usually enough to keep this dog clean and comfortable.

FUN FACT

After World War II (1939–1945), the Australian Shepherd's popularity skyrocketed when these dogs were shown in many films, on television and in rodeos and horse shows.

FAMOUS DOGS

The main character of the children's book *Henry the Dog with No Tail* is an Australian Shepherd. These dogs do have tails. They are just naturally short.

Bearded Collie

FUN FACT

The Beardie is also known as the Mountain Collie, Highland Collie or the Hairy Mou'ed Collie.

FAMOUS DOGS

The title role in the 2006 movie ***The Shaggy Dog*** was played by a Bearded Collie.

Appearance:
Height: 51 to 56 centimetres (20 to 22 inches)
Weight: 20 to 25 kilograms (45 to 55 pounds)

The Bearded Collie is a strong pastoral dog. He has a shaggy, waterproof double coat. Bearded Collie puppies are born with a mixture of dark and white fur. As they move into adulthood, the darker colour lightens. Bearded Collies are often confused with Old English Sheepdogs. A Bearded Collie has a much longer tail, however.

Personality: Owners describe the Bearded Collie's personality as humorous. This lively breed enjoys bouncing around and playing. Known for its "bounce", the Beardie has a high level of energy. Beardies also love children, but they can be a bit too rough for small children.

Breed Background: The Bearded Collie is one of the United Kingdom's oldest dog breeds. The breed was developed in the 1500s when a Polish sea captain made a trade with a Scottish shepherd. The shepherd then bred the Beardie with other herding and flock dogs, such as the Old English Sheepdog.

Country of Origin: Scotland

Training Notes: Beardies are strong-willed dogs. They need early training with socialization. This means meeting new people and other animals. Obedience training is recommended for Beardies because they are natural herders.

Care Notes: This long-haired breed needs a fair amount of grooming. Weekly brushing keeps tangles from forming. The Bearded Collie needs extra attention when it is shedding. The breed also needs a bath every six to eight weeks.

FUN FACT

The name "Bearded" comes from the long hairs that grow on the dog's chin.

Beauceron

FUN FACT

The French also refer to this breed as *Bas Rouge*, which means Red Stockings.

Appearance:
Height: 63 to 70 centimetres (25 to 28 inches)
Weight: 29 to 39 kilograms (65 to 85 pounds)

The Beauceron has a short, smooth coat. The hair is slightly longer on the dog's neck, tail and backside. Most Beaucerons are black and tan. Some also have grey patches.

Personality: This devoted breed will work hard to please its owner. Beaucerons also have a strong instinct to protect their families.

Breed Background: Like many herding dogs, Beaucerons were developed to drive sheep and cattle. The Beauceron originated from the French Plains of Beauce.

Country of Origin: France

Training Notes: Training this intelligent breed is easy but important. Owners who do not properly train their Beaucerons can end up with a domineering pet.

Care Notes: Beaucerons are happiest when they have a purpose. These active dogs need to exercise both their bodies and their brains regularly. Organised activities, such as agility, are ideal for this breed.

Belgian Shepherd Dog (Groenendael)

Appearance:

Height: 56 to 66 centimetres (22 to 26 inches)
Weight: 18 to 34 kilograms (40 to 75 pounds)

The Groenendael has long, black hair. Some dogs have a black coat with white patches. This breed's double coat is shorter on its head, ears and lower legs.

Personality: Groenendaels can make confident, devoted companions. Groenendaels love to feel like they have a purpose or job to do.

Breed Background: The four varieties of Belgian Shepherd Dogs are all named according to their Belgian region of origin. Professor Adolphe Reul of the Belgian Veterinary School named them.

Country of Origin: Belgium

Training Notes: Similar to the Malinois, the Groenendael needs early training. These dogs are smart and quick learners. They are also commonly trained as police military dogs or for search-and-rescue work.

Care Notes: The Groenendael sheds year-round. It needs to be brushed weekly. This dog also needs adequate exercise, both mental and physical.

FUN FACT

During World War I (1914–1918), Belgian Sheepdogs worked on the battlefields as message carriers and ambulance dogs.

Belgian Shepherd Dog (Malinois)

FUN FACT

The Belgian Malinois often runs in large circles. This habit comes from the breed's herding instinct.

Appearance:
Height: 56 to 66 centimetres (22 to 26 inches)
Weight: 27 to 29 kilograms (60 to 65 pounds)

The Malinois (*MAL-in-wah*) has a black muzzle and ears. Its main coat colour is a shade of red, fawn or grey.

Personality: This breed loves its human family. It takes time to warm up to strangers, however. The Belgian Malinois does well with older children.

Breed Background: The Belgian Malinois was developed as a sheepherder. Today members of this breed are best known for their work as police and military dogs.

Country of Origin: Belgium

Training Notes: The Belgian Malinois needs consistent training. Pups especially need socialization during their first six months of life.

Care Notes: The Belgian Malinois's short coat makes grooming a simple task. These dogs do shed though. Regular brushing can help keep dead hair off carpets and furniture.

Bergamasco

Appearance:
Height: 56 to 62 centimetres (22 to 25 inches)
Weight: 26 to 38 kilograms (57 to 84 pounds)

The Bergamasco has a long, harsh coat. The hair varies in colour from grey to black. Looking rather messy, the hair falls across the dog's eyes. It actually protects the animal's sight, though. This herding dog works high in the mountains where the sun glares off the snow.

Personality: The Bergamasco is known for its loyalty and love of children. These rare dogs make excellent watchdogs and family pets. They have a strong protective instinct.

Country of Origin: Italy

Training Notes: This smart breed has a strong personality. It needs an owner who is willing to put time and effort into training. Since most Bergamascos are wary of strangers, early socialization is also important.

Care Notes: The Bergamasco's heavy coat makes it a poor match for owners in warmer climates. These dogs thrive in cooler areas. A Bergamasco needs lots of exercise and prefers a countryside environment.

FUN FACT

When this breed is about a year old, a groomer should section its rough hair into cords. The process takes a lot of time. It never has to be done again, though.

Border Collie

FUN FACT

A herding Border Collie often walks in a crouched position. He looks like a cat hunting prey when it does this.

Appearance:
Height: 46 to 58 centimetres (18 to 23 inches)
Weight: 14 to 20 kilograms (30 to 45 pounds)

Border Collies come in a variety of colours and patterns. A Border Collie can have a medium-length coat or a short, smooth coat. Common colours for Border Collies are black and white, but there are 50 colour variations.

Personality: Border Collies are best known for their intelligence and high energy. Due to their tendency to herd, Border Collies do best with older children.

Breed Background: The Border Collie is named for its area of origin. This dog was developed between England, Scotland and Wales and was used for working sheep in the hills and mountains.

Country of Origin:
United Kingdom

Training Notes: If not properly trained, these dogs can become destructive. Early socialization and crate training are important for Border Collies. These dogs can also be trained for mountain rescue work.

Care Notes: Border Collies need a lot of physical exercise. They also require mental stimulation. Canine sports, such as fetch, can help satisfy both these needs.

Briard

Appearance:

Height: 56 to 69 centimetres (22 to 27 inches)
Weight: 23 to 45 kilograms (50 to 100 pounds)

The Briard has long fur covering its body and face, varying in shades of blacks and fawn. These dogs are also known for having double dewclaws on the hind legs.

Personality: Briards make wonderful family pets. They are loyal, love children and want to be part of all household activities. Briards love to engage in games.

Country of Origin: France

Training Notes: Briards are very independent, so owners need patience when teaching this breed commands. These dogs tend to be suspicious of strangers, so early socialization is important.

Care Notes: Briard owners must be willing to brush their dogs every other day. Tanglesform quickly in this breed's long hair.

FUN FACT

Briards are sometimes used by armies as pack dogs, among other duties.

FUN FACT

In 1907, millionaire banker J.P. Morgan bought a champion Collie called Wishaw Clinker. He paid £2,800 for the dog. Today that would be like spending £69,000 on a Collie.

Collie (Rough)

Appearance:
Height: 51 to 61 centimetres (20 to 24 inches)
Weight: 23 to 34 kilograms (50 to 75 pounds)

The Collie is a lean, strong dog. Its **muzzle** is rounded and tapered. Sometimes a Collie will have one blue eye and one brown eye. But most Collies have dark brown eyes.

Collies come in a variety of colours, including **sable**, black and tan, and white. Many Collies have long, thick double coats, such as the Rough Collie. Other members of the breed have shorter, smooth coats.

Personality: Collies are known for their extreme devotion. Though independent, they share a deep bond with their human family members. These dogs are sweet and sensitive. Collies are also known for their intelligence. They behave well with other animals and with children.

Breed Background: The Collie's self-direction was considered a plus in its development. These herding dogs didn't just follow commands – they thought for themselves.

Country of Origin: Scotland

Training Notes: Collies are intelligent and easily trained. They are good listeners too. Gentle, positive training works best with these dogs. Collies need socialization so they do not become afraid of strangers.

Care Notes: Owners should never give a Collie a common medication called ivermectin. Found in many **heartworm** pills, this drug can make Collies seriously ill. The medicine also has the same effect on Australian Shepherds, Shetland Sheepdogs and Old English Sheepdogs. A Collie needs plenty of daily exercise. This dog's long hair should be brushed weekly.

FUN FACT

The Collie is well-known for its role in the *Lassie* films, featuring a Rough Collie as the main character.

FUN FACT

Finnish Lapphunds were first bred to be dark-coloured so they would stand out in the snow.

Finnish Lapphund

Appearance:
Height: 44 to 49 centimetres (18 to 19 inches)
Weight: 15 to 24 kilograms (33 to 53 pounds)

The Finnish Lapphund comes in many colours. The most common are black and brown. Lappies, as they are sometimes called, can also have tan or white markings. The breed's long double coat protects it from the cold.

Personality: Many people see the Finnish Lapphund as the perfect pet. Lappies are calm and friendly with people. Their gentle temperament makes them great matches for families with children.

Breed Background: The Finnish Lapphund was developed for hard work in cold temperatures, such as herding reindeer.

Country of Origin: Finland

Training Notes: The Finnish Lapphund is eager to learn and quick to train. When properly trained, these dogs get along well with other animals.

Care Notes: This breed is born with a soft coat that requires a lot of grooming. As the dog gets older, the coat becomes rougher. Weekly brushings will help keep a Lapphund's coat looking its best.

German Shepherd Dog

Appearance:
Height: 58 to 63 centimetres (23 to 25 inches)
Weight: 34 to 43 kilograms (75 to 95 pounds)

German Shepherd Dogs are one of the most recognizable breeds. Their coats come in a wide range of colours and patterns. Most members of the breed have a black saddle with gold or tan hair on other parts of the body.

Personality: German Shepherds are loyal animals and make good family pets. They are known for calmly greeting people and for being well-behaved if properly trained.

Country of Origin: Germany

Training Notes: The German Shepherd is considered one of the smartest dog breeds. Training this breed is easy. An untrained German Shepherd, however, can be mischievous. Its bite is stronger than nearly all other dog breeds'.

Care Notes: Grooming a German Shepherd Dog isn't difficult. The breed does shed heavily though. Regular brushing can keep loose hair off owners and their belongings.

FUN FACT

German Shepherd Dogs are used by police and the military. During World War I (1914–1918), over 48,000 German Shepherds were enlisted in the German army.

FAMOUS DOGS

A German Shepherd called Rin Tin Tin appeared in silent films in the 1920s. The character would later be played by two of the original dog's descendants on television.

Hungarian Kuvasz

FUN FACT

Although the Kuvasz is pure white in colour, its skin is highly pigmented with patches of grey.

Appearance:
Height: 66 to 75 centimetres (26 to 30 inches)
Weight: 30 to 52 kilograms (66 to 115 pounds)

The Kuvasz has a slightly wavy double coat. The fur is typically short and smooth on its head, muzzle and ears and fine and woolly on the undercoat. The Kuvasz is pure white in colour.

Personality: The Kuvasz is a devoted and gentle companion dog and is suitable as a family pet. This breed is known for its patience. However, sometimes a Kuvasz is wary of strangers.

Breed Background: It is believed that the Kuvasz played an important part in the history of kingdoms and empires that flourished throughout Europe five to eight centuries ago.

Country of Origin: Hungary

Training Notes: The Kuvasz needs a firm hand with training, coupled with attention and companionship in order to properly socialize it in the home.

Care Notes: Because these dogs are natural herders, they should be kept in a fenced area for their protection. Its wavy, thick coat can withstand extreme cold weather, and it should be brushed reguarly.

Hungarian Puli

Appearance:
Height: 37 to 44 centimetres (15 to 18 inches)
Weight: 10 to 15 kilograms (22 to 33 pounds)

The Hungarian Puli stands out in any crowd. Its corded fur makes the dog look like a giant mop. These cords protect the dog from harsh weather. Though some dogs are white or grey, most members of this breed are black.

Personality: Pulik, the plural of Puli, are quite lively. They love being the centre of attention. They can make good pets for people with older children. They may be wary of strangers though.

Country of Origin: Hungary

Training Notes:
Pulik are highly intelligent and trainable. They do best when training begins early and remains consistent throughout adulthood.

Care Notes: Pulik are active animals and need daily exercise. Grooming them also takes effort and time. It can take an entire day for a dog to fully dry from a bath.

FUN FACT

The Pulik, or Drovers, have been an essential part of the lives of Hungarian shepherds for more than a century.

Komondor

FUN FACT

It is belived that he Komondor has been native to Hungary, a sheep and cattle country, longer than any other pastoral breed.

Appearance:

Height: 60 to 80 centimetres (24 to 32 inches)
Weight: 36 to 61 kilograms (80 to 135 pounds)

The Komondor's hair clings together like tassels, giving it a corded appearance. But underneath those white tassels is one strong and powerful animal. The dog's coat alone can weigh 7 kilograms (15 pounds)!

Personality: The Komondor is not overly affectionate. It is an excellent guard dog and is highly protective of its human family members. This breed has even been known to protect other animals in its household.

Country of Origin: Hungary

Training Notes: This breed can be independent and stubborn, so owners should begin training a Komondor at a young age.

Care Notes: Owners should learn how to care for a Komondor's coat from an experienced breeder or groomer. These dogs need a fair amount of playtime and exercise, and plenty of countryside in which to roam.

Norwegian Buhund

FUN FACT

Bu in Norwegian means "homestead", so ***Buhund*** is the "dog found on the homestead or farm".

Appearance:

Height: 41 to 45 centimetres (16 to 18 inches)
Weight: 12 to 18 kilograms (26 to 40 pounds)

The Norwegian Buhund comes in four colours: wheaten, which is yellow-brown, black, red and wolf-sable. A Buhund may also have a black mask or white markings.

Personality: This fearless, friendly breed stands out for its strong desire to please its owners. The Norwegian Buhund loves people, including children.

Breed Background:

The Buhund is a Spitz breed. Spitz dogs all descended from dogs in the Arctic region. A Spitz has dense fur, pointed ears and a pointed snout.

Country of Origin: Norway

Training Notes: The Buhund can be independent, but this dog learns quickly. Basic obedience and socialization training is also important from a young age.

Care Notes: This breed has a lot of energy. A Norwegian Buhund must run and play each day. Its coat is easy to care for, requiring occasional brushing and bathing.

Old English Sheepdog

FUN FACT

The Old English Sheepdog has a unique **gait**. It runs in much the same way as a bear does.

FAMOUS DOGS

In Disney's ***The Little Mermaid***, Prince Eric owns an Old English Sheepdog called Max.

Appearance:
Height: 56 to 61 centimetres (22 to 24 inches)
Weight: 27 to 41 kilograms (60 to 90 pounds)

The first thing anyone notices about the Old English Sheepdog is its wild, fluffy coat. Its coat is hard and **textured**. It is also waterproof. Although it comes in several colours, the hair is usually grey, grizzle or blue.

The Old English Sheepdog is a strong, large dog. It is very muscular. Some grow to be over 45 kilograms (100 pounds)!

Personality: This breed is known for its hoarse bark. Because these dogs are so big, children may try to ride them. This isn't safe for either the child or the dog. As long as children understand how to properly treat this friendly animal, an Old English Sheepdog can make an ideal family pet.

The Old English Sheepdog has a strong herding instinct. It may try to herd people. But early training can help this problem.

Country of Origin: England

Training Notes: Obedience training is a must, due to the breed's large size and level of energy. But do not overwork an Old English Sheepdog. Because bone growth continues for the first year and a half of their lives, these dogs are more likely to suffer an injury during early training.

Care Notes: Old English Sheepdogs need lots of care and attention. Owners must spend about three to four hours each week on grooming. These dogs can develop skin problems if they are not brushed often enough. This energetic breed also needs about two hours of exercise each day. They love to go for jogs with their owners.

FUN FACT

The Old English Sheepdog is sometimes called the Bobtail. This is because it is born without a tail.

Samoyed

FUN FACT

Samoyeds were not always pure white. When Samoyeds were first brought to Britain, explorers described these dogs as being both black and white.

Appearance:
Height: 46 to 56 centimetres (18 to 22 inches)
Weight: 16 to 29 kilograms (35 to 65 pounds)

The Samoyed's fluffy, white coat makes it easy to distinguish from other breeds. These dogs also look like they are smiling.

Personality: What sets this dog apart from other breeds most is its personality. Samoyeds are highly vocal. They tend to bark, howl and even seem to sing. A Sammie's singing sounds like varying pitches of prolonged howling.

Country of Origin: Russia

Training Notes: Samoyeds need training because of their high energy level. Excited dogs can be disobedient.

Care Notes: Samoyeds do not want to be inside all the time. They love spending time outdoors, especially in the snow. Their long coats need to be brushed weekly.

Shetland Sheepdog

Appearance:

Height: 35 to 37 centimetres (14 to 15 inches)
Weight: roughly 9 kilograms (20 pounds)

Shetland Sheepdogs, or Shelties, have long double coats. They come in a variety of colours. Sable, tricolour, blue merle, black and white, and white are among the most popular.

Personality: Shetland Sheepdogs are affectionate and responsive to their owners. However, sometimes they are wary of strangers.

Breed Background: The breed was developed on the Shetland Islands, north-east of Scotland.

Country of Origin: Scotland

Training Notes: Shetlanders are among the smartest dog breeds and are easy to train. Shetlanders may bark and try to herd people. Basic socialization and command training should begin early on.

Care Notes: Shetlanders have a lot of energy. They like to play and tend to bark frequently. Active families are often the best matches for these dogs. Shetlanders are heavy shedders. Regular brushing is important. Brushing also helps prevents matting, which can cause skin problems in this breed.

FUN FACT

A dog called Loggie was the first Shetlander to appear at Crufts in 1906. Crufts is held annually in the UK.

Swedish Vallhund

FUN FACT

The Swedish Vallhund is also called the Swedish Cattle Dog.

Appearance:
Height: 31 to 35 centimetres (12 to 14 inches)
Weight: 11 to 16 kilograms (25 to 35 pounds)

The Swedish Vallhund's low body, short coat and perky ears make it look like a Corgi. These dogs come in combinations of grey, red or yellow. White markings are also common on Swedish Vallhunds.

Personality: The Swedish Vallhund enjoys being on the go. These dogs are ideal for active people and will take all the exercise given. They are also friendly, alert and excellent guard dogs.

Breed Background: The Swedish Vallhund nearly died out in Sweden in the 1930s.

Country of Origin: Sweden

Training Notes: Swedish Vallhunds are easy to train. It is important to keep the tone positive though. This breed does not respond well to loud voices.

Care Notes: The Swedish Vallhund needs a lot of exercise. The breed loves long walks. Owners can also take this breed along when hiking. Its short coat requires occasional brushing and bathing.

Welsh Corgi (Cardigan)

Appearance:

Height: 25 to 33 centimetres (10 to 13 inches)
Weight: 11 to 17 kilograms (25 to 38 pounds)

The Cardigan Welsh Corgi stands low to the ground. While not tall, the Corgi is definitely long. They measure roughly 1 metre (3.3 feet) from nose to tail. The Cardigan's coat is short and weatherproof.

Personality: The Cardigan is a small dog with a big personality. It is driven and determined. It gets along well with older children and makes a pleasant pet. He may try to herd young children, however.

Country of Origin: Wales

Training Notes: Cardigans are smart and easily trained. They are natural guardians, so socialization is important during early training.

Care Notes: A Corgi has more back problems than many other breeds due to its long, low back. Owners should not allow a Corgi to jump off a bed or other furniture. For exercise, a Corgi loves daily walks. Its short coat should be groomed regularly.

FUN FACT

The Cardigan's low height is helpful in herding. If a cow tries to kick the animal, chances are good that its hoof will go right over this dog's body!

Welsh Corgi (Pembroke)

FUN FACT

The easiest way to tell the difference between this breed and the Cardigan is looking at their tails – the Pembroke has a much shorter, or docked, tail.

FAMOUS DOGS

Queen Elizabeth II has owned more than 30 Pembrokes during her reign.

Appearance:
Height: 25 to 30 centimetres (10 to 12 inches)
Weight: up to 12 kilograms (26 pounds)

The Pembroke's body is about one and a half times as long as it is tall. It is low to the ground and has short legs.

The Pembroke is a double-coated breed. The inner coat is short and thick with longer, coarser hair over it. The Pembroke's coat varies in colour. It can be red, sable, fawn or black and tan. Pembrokes sometimes have markings on their legs and neck.

Personality: Pembrokes are highly intelligent, loyal and willing to please their owners. They are also good with children. They do tend to bark, however. Pembrokes are natural watchdogs.

The Pembroke has a lot of confidence for such a little dog. Perhaps that is why this breed was used to herd cattle. However, these dogs love their family members and make great pets.

Breed Background: The Pembroke was bred out from the Cardigan Welsh Corgi. Both Corgi varieties are descendants of the Keeshond, Pomeranian, Schipperkes and the Swedish Vallhund. Corgis were used as cattle drivers, **vermin** hunters and farm guards.

Country of Origin: Wales

Training Notes: These smart dogs are eager to learn new things and to please their owners. Pembrokes also respond well to mental challenges, such as playing fetch.

Care Notes: Exercise is important for this lively breed. Pembrokes should be kept on a sensible canine diet. This breed is prone to weight gain if owners overfeed their dogs or give them human food.

Their soft, waterproof coat is easy to groom. It needs brushing and bathing only when necessary.

FUN FACT

The Pembroke typically has straighter legs than the Cardigan Welsh Corgi.

Other pastoral breeds

Belgian Shepherd Dog (Tervueren)

Appearance:
Height: 56 to 66 centimetres (22 to 26 inches)
Weight: 26 to 42 kilograms (57 to 93 pounds)
Known for: being closely related to the Belgian Sheepdog
Country of Origin: Belgium

Picardy Sheepdog

Appearance:
Height: 55 to 65 centimetres (22 to 26 inches)
Weight: 25 to 35 kilograms (55 to 77 pounds)
Known for: performing well in the show ring
Country of Origin: France

Polish Lowland Sheepdog ▶

Appearance:
Height: 42 to 50 centimetres (17 to 20 inches)
Weight: 22 to 30 kilograms (49 to 66 pounds)
Known for: fearlessly protecting their flocks from predators
Country of Origin: Poland

Pyrenean Sheepdog (Long Haired) ▼

Appearance:

Height: 40 to 48 centimetres (16 to 19 inches)
Weight: 20 to 28 kilograms (44 to 62 pounds)

Known for: living in the Pyrenees Mountains for centuries

Countries of Origin: France and Spain

Independent terriers

The Kennel Club's Terrier group is made up of 27 dog breeds. Terriers were first developed as hunting dogs. Many of them worked alongside larger hunting dogs, such as hounds. The hounds chased foxes and other burrowing animals into their dens. The terriers' job was to force **quarry** out of these tight spaces. Some terriers still perform this work.

Many members of the terrier group are popular as pets. These high-energy canines are known for their feisty personalities. They need owners who are prepared to train these intelligent yet independent animals. Pet terriers need lots of exercise and engaging activities.

Terriers have a distinctive, spirited personality. They typically have a low **tolerance** for other animals, including other dogs. Terriers should never be kept in the same home with small pets, such as mice or hamsters.

Terriers come in a wide range of sizes and appearances. Don't let the littlest group members fool you, however. Every member of the terrier group shares at least some of that determined terrier spirit. Get ready for a look at each one!

FUN FACT

The Kennel Club runs many education campaigns to help ensure people buy the right breed, from the right breeder, and it lobbies for legislative changes that will help dogs.

FUN FACT

The Airedale Terrier aided the Red Cross during times of war.

Airedale Terrier

Appearance:
Height: 56 to 61 centimetres (22 to 24 inches)
Weight: 23 to 27 kilograms (50 to 60 pounds)

The Airedale Terrier is known as the King of Terriers. It is the largest of all the terrier breeds. It has a double-layered coat. The wiry hair is tan with black around the dog's body and neck.

Personality: Few dogs possess a wider range of traits than the Airedale Terrier. This breed is often described as playful to the point of being silly. At the same time, Airedales make excellent guard dogs. Some even served as military dogs in World War I (1914–1918).

Breed Background: The Airedale Terrier is thought to have originated in England in the Aire River Valley. It was developed by crossing a Terrier with an Otterhound.

Country of Origin: England

Training Notes: The Airedale Terrier becomes bored easily. Owners must be ready to provide these intelligent animals with plenty of positive training and exercise.

Care Notes: Airedale Terriers aren't heavy shedders. However, owners must hand-strip their dogs three to four times per year. By pulling at the coat in a special way, they remove the dead hair. These dogs also enjoy daily exercise, including walks.

Bedlington Terrier

FUN FACT

The Bedlington Terrier was once known as the Rothbury Terrier.

Appearance:

Height: 41 to 43 centimetres (22 to 16 inches)
Weight: 23 to 27 kilograms (50 to 60 pounds)

The Bedlington Terrier looks like a lamb, but he is a terrier through and through. Its coat is thick and soft and comes in blue, liver or sandy.

Personality: This breed is playful and affectionate. Often called a "little powerhouse", it is brave and energetic. It makes a great family companion and is fairly friendly with strangers. Typically it can get along well with other dogs if properly trained at a young age. Bedlingtons do like to bark, too.

Breed Background: The Bedlington Terrier hails from the former mining regions in northern England. He takes its name from the Bedlington Mining Shire.

Country of Origin: England

Training Notes: These dogs are fast runners and need to be taught to come back when called. Behavioural problems can arise if they do not have enough physical and mental stimulation.

Care Notes: Only let this dog off a lead in an enclosed area. It will chase anything that catches its attention! Bedlingtons need plenty of exercise, such as a daily, long walk. Its coat does not shed much, but it should be brushed and bathed regularly. This breed works well with people who have allergies because a Bedlington is **hypoallergenic.**

Border Terrier

FUN FACT

The Border Terrier's **breed standard** describes the dog's head as "like that of an otter".

Appearance:
Height: 25 to 28 centimetres (10 to 11 inches)
Weight: 5 to 7 kilograms (11 to 16 pounds)

The Border Terrier has a short, wiry coat. Its coat colour comes in several varieties, such as wheaten, red, grizzle and tan or blue and tan.

Personality: Border Terriers are affectionate dogs and love spending time with their favourite humans. However, they can be easily excited and may bark often.

Breed Background: In the 1800s Borders were used to hunt foxes, otters and even badgers. The breed barks to drive wild animals from their dens. It was once known as the Reedwater or the Coquetdale Terrier.

Countries of Origin:
Scotland, England

Training Notes: Border Terriers learn quickly and respond well to obedience training. Owners should keep training fun as this breed gets bored easily.

Care Notes: A sturdy fence is a must. Borders are skilled escape artists. Their coats are easy to maintain with scissors for quick trims to tidy up their appearance. Their weatherproof coats require occasional brushing.

Bull Terrier

▲
FAMOUS DOGS

Bullseye, the mascot for the US retailer Target, is a Bull Terrier. The red circles around her left eye are safe vegetable dye and are only placed on her face for advertisements.

Appearance:

Height: 53 to 56 centimetres (21 to 22 inches)
Weight: 23 to 32 kilograms (50 to 70 pounds)

Bull Terriers have a unique look. Some people describe the Bull Terrier's head as egg-shaped. The dog is also said to have a Roman nose, which means it has a high bridge. The Bull Terrier has eyes shaped like triangles. Its short, glossy coat comes in many colour variations.

Personality: These active dogs are known for their fun personalities. With proper obedience training, Bull Terriers do well in homes with younger children. He may not get along well with other dogs, however.

Country of Origin: England

Training Notes: The Bull Terrier's intelligence is a plus for training. This breed responds best to training when motivated by toys or treats.

Care Notes: Daily exercise is important for Bull Terriers. They require occasional grooming with a soft brush or a hound glove, which is a mitt with brush bristles.

FUN FACT

A smaller dog called the Miniature Bull Terrier is considered a separate breed. The only difference between the two breeds is its size.

Bull Terrier (Miniature)

FUN FACT

Miniature Bull Terriers are more prone to slipped patella, which is the dislocation of the kneecaps. Maintaining a healthy weight can help with this problem.

Appearance:

Height: 25 to 33 centimetres (10 to 14 inches)
Weight: 11 to 15 kilograms (24 to 33 pounds)

Like its cousin the Bull Terrier, this dog is a strongly built, muscular breed. The Miniature Bull Terrier has a black nose, almond-shaped eyes and small, thin ears. It can be all white, black, red or fawn.

Personality: The Miniature Bull Terrier is a loyal and obedient dog. It is considered fun-loving and almost downright clownish. This breed will become very attached to its owners.

Breed Background: The Miniature Bull Terrier has the same standards as the Bull Terrier. But the miniature version was developed to be a more manageable size.

Country of Origin: England

Training Notes: Miniature Bull Terriers do not do well if left along for more than eight hours a day. It needs physical and mental exercise. This breed also does well with firm and consistent training.

Care Notes: The Miniature Bull Terrier needs a lot of exercise and daily running. It is easy to groom, only requiring an occasional combing and bathing.

Cairn Terrier

Appearance:
Height: 28 to 30 centimetres (11 to 12 inches)
Weight: 6 to 7 kilograms (14 to 16 pounds)

Cairn Terriers are built for the outdoors. Their wiry coats resist water and protect the dogs from harsh weather.

Personality: Cairn Terriers are little dogs with big personalities. These tiny canines are as brave, smart and confident as many larger breeds. They're also not afraid to demand attention from their owners.

Breed Background: The Cairn Terrier is the smallest of the Scottish terriers. These terriers were developed to hunt rodents. Cairns are piles of stones used as tombstones in Scotland. The Cairn Terrier got its name by driving rats and other tiny creatures out of these rock piles.

Country of Origin: Scotland

Training Notes: The Cairn Terrier is highly intelligent and can learn quickly. However, even the best-trained Cairns cannot be trusted to obey off a lead because they tend to be independent.

Care Notes: This breed should be exercised regularly to stay busy and to release energy. Its coat should be brushed regularly.

FUN FACT

Cairn Terriers come in every colour except white. White dogs are a separate breed – the West Highland White Terrier.

FAMOUS DOGS

Dorothy's dog, Toto, from the *Wizard of Oz*, is a Cairn Terrier. The female dog that played the role was called Terry.

Dandie Dinmont Terrier

FUN FACT

The Dandie Dinmont is the only breed named after a fictional character. The name came from Sir Walter Scott's novel *Guy Mannering*. The character Mr Dandie Dinmont owned small Scottish terriers.

FAMOUS DOGS

Queen Victoria owned a Dandie Dinmont Terrier.

Appearance:

Height: 20 to 28 centimetres (8 to 11 inches)
Weight: 8 to 11 kilograms (18 to 24 pounds)

The Dandie Dinmont Terrier has a large, fluffy head. Its coat contains a mixture of soft and hard hairs. The Dandie Dinmont comes in either mustard, which is a yellow-tan, or pepper, which is a black and white mix.

Personality: Dandie Dinmont Terriers aren't as excitable as some other small dogs. They love to cuddle with their favourite humans.

Breed Background: The Dandie Dinmont was developed in the Cheviot Hills between England and Scotland in the 1600s. The breed may have been developed from the Skye Terrier and the now-extinct Scotch Terrier. The Dandie Dinmont Terrier was popular among gypsies and was used by farmers to kill vermin. With its short legs, it was also able to hunt badger and otters.

Countries of Origin: Scotland, England

Training Notes: If an owner wants a Dandie with a mild personality, training is important. They aren't the most obedient of pets. However, they are not difficult to train if you are firm and consistent. Dandie owners will get the best results with positive, rewards-based training.

Care Notes: Daily exercise, such as playing in a fenced area or a walk on a lead, is important. They also enjoy running in safe, open areas.

This breed needs a large amount of grooming, including regular brushing. It is recommended that Dandie Dinmont Terriers go to a professional groomer. Dead hair should be plucked out once or twice per year.

FUN FACT

The Dandie Dinmont Terrier is sometimes also called the Hindlee Terrier.

Fox Terrier (Smooth)

FUN FACT

While the Fox Terrier is a medium-sized dog, its teeth are surprisingly large. They are the same size of a Doberman Pinscher's teeth.

Appearance:
Height: 33 to 41 centimetres (13 to 16 inches)
Weight: 7 to 9 kilograms (15 to 19 pounds)

The Smooth Fox Terrier has a short, smooth coat. It is mostly white with black or tan markings.

Personality: The Smooth Fox Terrier is known for being entertaining and playful. It wants to spend as much time as possible with its family. Left alone too long, this breed can develop behaviour problems quickly.

Breed Background: As its name suggests, Smooth Fox Terriers were developed to hunt foxes. Working alongside hounds, these smaller canines could go where the larger dogs could not – in the ground. When the hounds chased a fox into its hole, the terriers would go into the hole and chase the quarry back out.

Country of Origin: England

Training Notes: Training a Smooth Fox Terrier can begin at an early age because of its instinct to hunt. These dogs are intelligent and can learn tricks easily.

Care Notes: Grooming a Smooth Fox Terrier is easy but important. The breed's smooth coat doesn't mat. But it does shed heavily twice per year. Weekly brushings can greatly reduce the amount of fur that ends up on carpets and furniture.

Fox Terrier (Wire)

Appearance:
Height: 33 to 41 centimetres (13 to 16 inches)
Weight: 7 to 9 kilograms (15 to 19 pounds)

The Wire Fox Terrier shares many traits with the Smooth Fox Terrier. In fact, the only difference between the two breeds is coat texture. A Wire Fox Terrier's dense, wiry coat is mostly white in colour with black or tan markings.

Personality: Like their smooth cousins, Wire Fox Terriers are energetic dogs. It doesn't take much to get them moving. Slowing them down, on the other hand, may seem impossible. This lively breed thrives on activity.

Breed Background:
Originally known as the Rough-Haired Terrier, these dogs were bred in the 1800s for hunting fox, rats and other small rodents.

Country of Origin: England

Training Notes: Wire Fox Terriers are highly trainable with positive reinforcement. Like many other terriers, Wire Fox Terriers are independent, so owners must be consistent.

Care Notes: Wire Fox Terriers living in small spaces must get outside for daily exercise. A quick walk won't do. These terriers want to play! It requires only occasional brushing and bathing.

FUN FACT

The Wire Fox Terrier's tail doesn't wag like other dog's tails. Instead, it quivers – moving just slightly back and forth.

Glen Of Imaal Terrier

FUN FACT

Glen of Imaal Terriers mature slower than many other breeds. Glens often aren't considered adults until they are three or four years old.

Appearance:
Height: 30 to 36 centimetres (12 to 14 inches)
Weight: up to 16 kilograms (35 pounds)

The Glen of Imaal Terrier has a medium-length double coat. The hair comes in several shades, including wheaten, blue or brindle. The colour brindle means brown with streaks of another colour.

Personality: Glens adore their owners. They want to be with people as much as possible. At the same time, these dogs aren't nearly as demanding as other terrier breeds.

Breed Background: The Glen of Imaal Terrier is named for a glen, or valley, in Ireland's Wicklow Mountains. The Irish Kennel Club recognised the breed in 1934. But it would be decades before the Kennel Club of England would follow.

Country of Origin: Ireland

Training Notes: Glens learn quickly. They also bore quickly. The key to training this breed is keeping the sessions short and interesting.

Care Notes: Glen of Imaal Terriers need a surprising amount of exercise and stimulation. Owners should be prepared to go for long walks and play plenty of games. They must also be patient when it comes to locating a puppy. Because there aren't many breeders, waiting lists are common.

Irish Terrier

FUN FACT

The Irish Terrier earned its nickname the "Red Devil" from its relentless pursuit of quarry.

Appearance:

Height: 38 to 48 centimetres (15 to 19 inches)
Weight: 11 to 12 kilograms (25 to 27 pounds)

At first glance the Irish Terrier looks a lot like the Airedale Terrier. The biggest difference is size. The Irish Terrier is smaller than the Airedale. The Irish Terrier is also red instead of black and tan.

Personality: Like most other terriers, the Irish Terrier's hunting instinct is strong. These dogs are also highly affectionate and protective. It is also great with children and makes an excellent family companion.

Country of Origin: Ireland

Training Notes: The Irish Terrier is intelligent yet requires patience to train. Even after this dog learns commands, its owners must be consistent and practise them often with the dog.

Care Notes: Irish Terriers need their wiry coats brushed regularly. Owners must be willing to provide these dogs with plenty of exercise, such as daily walks.

Kerry Blue Terrier

FUN FACT

Kerry Blue Terriers are born black and can take up to 18 months to change to blue.

Appearance:
Height: 46 to 51 centimetres (18 to 20 inches)
Weight: 15 to 18 kilograms (33 to 40 pounds)

The Kerry Blue Terrier is best known for its blue-grey coat. The breed also sports a distinctive mop of hair and beard that give its face a unique shape.

Personality: These dogs love people. They get along well with both adults and children. When strangers come around, however, they may become protective. Kerry Blue Terriers make excellent guard dogs.

While no terrier can be trusted with small animals, this breed isn't a good choice for a multi-pet household.

Breed Background: The Kerry Blue Terrier originated in the 1700s and was developed in County Kerry, Ireland. The Kerry Blue Terrier is the national dog of Ireland. It is a descendant of the Portuguese Water Dog, the Soft-Coated Wheaten Terrier and possibly the Irish Wolfhound. The Kerry Blue Terrier was and still is used for farm herding and police work.

Country of Origin: Ireland

Training Notes: This breed is likely to act aggressively with other dogs. Socialization can instill good manners for when the Kerry Blue encounters other dogs in public. Still, owners should always remain watchful.

Care Notes: Keep a towel handy if you own this breed. The beard of hair absorbs a lot of water each time this dog has a drink. The Kerry Blue Terrier's non-shedding coat is hypoallergenic but still needs to be brushed weekly.

FUN FACT

Kerry Blue Terriers are sometimes called Irish Blue Terriers.

Lakeland Terrier

FUN FACT

The Lakeland Terrier is a talented tracker. Tracking means when a dog is able to locate a certain object using the object's scent.

FAMOUS DOGS

Champion Stingray of Derrybah won Best in Show at Crufts in 1967 and then became Best in Show at the USA's Westminster the following year. Its trophy is housed at the Kennel Club in London.

Appearance:

Height: 30 to 37 centimetres (12 to 15 inches)
Weight: 7 to 8 kilograms (15 to 17 pounds)

The Lakeland Terrier has a dense, weatherproof coat. The outer coat is hard and wiry. Its hair can be black and tan, blue and tan, red, wheaten, liver, blue or black. It is a small and sturdy dog.

Personality: Lakeland Terriers are cheerful and affectionate dogs. They love children and make an excellent guard dog. They especially love to guard their food and toys.

Breed Background: This breed comes from England's Lake District. It is one of the oldest Terrier breeds today.

Country of Origin: England

Training Notes: Early obedience training is a must with Lakeland Terriers, especially housebreaking. Early socialization may also help with this breed's aggression towards other dogs.

Care Notes: The Lakeland Terrier should have its coat plucked two times per year by pulling the old hair out by hand. It also enjoys daily exercise, such as a long walk or jog.

Manchester Terrier

Appearance:

Height: 38 to 41 centimetres (15 to 16 inches)
Weight: 5 to 10 kilograms (12 to 22 pounds)

A quick look might lead a person to mistake a Manchester Terrier for a small Doberman Pinscher. Their coats share the same black and tan colouration. Their pointed ears also make the animals look similar.

Personality: The Manchester's personality is all terrier. These little dogs are lively, loyal and intelligent. Like other terriers, the Manchester should be introduced slowly to other dogs and strangers. It is a devoted family member and can fit into any environment, town or countryside.

Country of Origin: England

Training Notes: Although this is a smart breed, many owners find Manchester Terriers difficult to house-train. Using a crate and sticking to a strict training schedule can help.

Care Notes: Owners must keep up with this energetic breed. Many find that organised activities, such as agility and rally events, help keep this breed entertained.

FUN FACT

The Manchester Terrier is the oldest known Terrier breed.

Norwich Terrier

FUN FACT

The Norwich Terrier and the Norfolk Terrier look a lot alike. The only difference is that the Norfolk Terrier has floppy ears instead of pointed ears.

Appearance:
Height: less than 25 centimetres (10 inches)
Weight: 5 to 6 kilograms (10 to 13 pounds)

The Norwich Terrier has short legs and a rough double coat. The hair comes in a variety of colours, including red, wheaten or black and tan. A combination of black and tan is among the most popular.

Personality: Norwich Terriers make great pets because they are friendly and loyal. This breed's small size can be deceiving, however. This friendly animal is no lapdog. The Norwich Terrier doesn't want to sit quietly and watch what's happening. He thrives on activity.

Breed Background: Developed in East Anglia, England, the Norwich Terrier and the Norfolk Terrier used to be the same breed. The two have been considered separate breeds since 1964.

Country of Origin: United Kingdom

Training Notes: Norwich Terriers are intelligent and easily trained. These dogs respond well to positive reinforcement, such as small treats.

Care Notes: This dog is highly active and requires a lot of daily exercise. A Norwich Terrier needs regular grooming. Like the Airedale Terrier, the Norwich's fur must be hand-stripped. Many owners find it easier to hire a groomer for this task.

Parson Russell Terrier

Appearance:

Height: 30 to 36 centimetres (12 to 14 inches)
Weight: 6 to 8 kilograms (13 to 17 pounds)

Commonly called the Jack Russell Terrier, the Parson Russell comes in two coat types: smooth and rough. Smooth dogs have short hair. The rough coat is a bit longer. Dogs with this coat type have shaggy eyebrows and short beards.

Personality: The Parson Russell Terrier is lively. The breed simply overflows with enthusiasm. Its high activity level makes many people adore the Parson Russell. All that energy is also the reason the breed is not for everyone.

Countries of Origin: England, United States

Training Notes: This smart dog is capable of learning many commands. Obedience training should begin when the terrier is a puppy.

Care Notes: The Parson Russell Terrier needs to run for at least 30 minutes each day. They are also talented escape artists. The breed is known for getting out of fenced gardens by digging under the fences. Many owners find that **earthdog trials** help fulfil the Parson Russell's needs for exercise, hunting and digging.

FUN FACT

Parson Russell Terriers can jump about five times their own height.

FAMOUS DOGS

Wishbone from the children's TV show of the same name is a Parson Russell Terrier.

Scottish Terrier

FUN FACT

George, the fourth Earl of Dumbarton, in Scotland, nicknamed the Scottish Terrier the "little diehard".

FAMOUS DOGS

Jock from the Disney film ***Lady and the Tramp*** is a Scottish Terrier.

Appearance:
Height: 23 to 28 centimetres (9 to 11 inches)
Weight: 8 to 10 kilograms (18 to 22 pounds)

Scottish Terriers have short, stocky bodies. He has a course, wiry coat. Although they come in several colours, including black, wheaten and brindle, black is the most common.

Personality: Scotties are known for their independence. They are playful as puppies, but they mature into dignified adults. But they are also gentle and loving with their human family members.

Breed Background: This dog was developed in Scotland in the 1700s. It was first called the Aberdeen Terrier.

Country of Origin: Scotland

Training Notes: Owners can teach this breed a number of commands. But a Scottish Terrier may ignore its training if it doesn't want to comply. Positive praise and rewards may help if this dog develops behavioural problems.

Care Notes: Scotties have a strong chase instinct. It is important to keep this breed on a lead in public for this reason. Even in the privacy of a garden, a fence is a good idea for most terriers. A single squirrel can set a Scottie off running.

Skye Terrier

FUN FACT

The Skye Terrier has also been called the Terrier of the Western Isles.

Appearance:

Height: 23 to 25 centimetres (9 to 10 inches)
Weight: 11 to 18 kilograms (25 to 40 pounds)

To people unfamiliar with the breed, the Skye Terrier may look like it needs a haircut. The hair on the breed's head is so long that it falls over the dog's eyes. Its coat is long and silky, flowing all the way to the ground.

Personality: Skye Terrier owners describe the breed as affectionate and loyal. These dogs aren't nearly as warm with new people, however. They are also uneasy around strange dogs.

Breed Background: Developed on the Isle of Skye, this brave little terrier hunted badgers, foxes and otters. He later became a popular pet for English nobility in the mid-1800s.

Country of Origin: Scotland

Training Notes: This breed needs early training and socialization. Puppies who are exposed to people will be more comfortable with them as adults.

Care Notes: Skye Terriers need about 30 minutes of exercise each day. A long, daily walk is ideal. Their long hair should be brushed a couple of times each week.

Soft-Coated Wheaten Terrier

FUN FACT

Wheaten Terriers change colour as they mature. Puppies are born a rusty brown. The blond, wheaten coat develops by the time a dog reaches adulthood.

Appearance:
Height: 43 to 48 centimetres (17 to 19 inches)
Weight: 14 to 18 kilograms (30 to 40 pounds)

This breed's name is no accident. The Soft-Coated Wheaten Terrier's fluffy, tan coat is as soft as silk. A Wheaten's fur also plays a big role in its appearance. The dog's hair hangs over its eyes. The breed also has a long beard.

Personality: Soft-Coated Wheaten Terriers offer owners a wide variety of traits. This breed is strong and energetic. Many people describe Wheatens as bouncing clowns. When they're not on the move, Wheaten Terriers love cuddling with their favourite humans.

Country of Origin: Ireland

Training Notes: This breed can be independent. Training works best with a consistent schedule and firm owner.

Care Notes: Grooming twice per week is necessary. This dog doesn't shed much fur, so owners must brush the dead hair out instead. They also need daily exercise, such as a walk.

Staffordshire Bull Terrier

FUN FACT

The Staffordshire Bull Terrier is known for its love and devotion to children in its household. It is nicknamed the "Nanny Dog" for this reason.

Appearance:
Height: 36 to 41 centimetres (14 to 16 inches)
Weight: 1 to 17 kilograms (24 to 38 pounds)

The Staffordshire Bull Terrier, or Staffie, has a smooth coat in several colour variations. It is commonly black, blue, red, fawn or white.

Personality: Staffordshire Bull Terriers are highly affectionate and loyal. Some people also describe these dogs as having a playful sense of humour. Staffies are also known for being obedient with their owners.

Breed Background: The Staffordshire Bull Terrier was developed in the 1800s by crossing a Bulldog and various local terriers of that time in England.

Country of Origin: England

Training Notes: Staffordshire Bull Terriers are known for their intelligence. Positive yet persistent training is a must for this breed.

Care Notes: A daily walk and play session are usually enough to keep this dog in good physical shape. Be sure to keep a Staffie on a lead at all times in public, however. The breed does not generally get along well with other dogs.

Welsh Terrier

FUN FACT

Because the Welsh Terrier barely sheds, many people who are allergic to dogs can tolerate it.

Appearance:

Height: 36 to 38 centimetres (14 to 15 inches)
Weight: 9 to 10 kilograms (19 to 21 pounds)

The Welsh Terrier looks a lot like the Airedale Terrier. Its tan and black double coat is wiry on the outside and soft underneath. But the Welsh Terrier is much smaller than the Airedale.

Personality: Most members of the Terrier group have a lot of energy and a fair amount of independence. Many terrier owners value these traits. For those who do not, however, the Welsh Terrier offers a gentler temperament. Welsh Terriers are calm and mild mannered. Still, they provide plenty of fun and entertainment. They are simply more willing to obey than many of their fellow terrier group members.

Country of Origin: Wales

Training Notes: Welsh Terriers are smart and easily trainable. Firm but positive training works best with these dogs.

Care Notes: Welsh Terriers need about an hour of exercise each day. A fenced garden works great for this breed. Its coat should be brushed regularly too.

West Highland White Terrier

Appearance:
Height: 25 to 28 centimetres (10 to 11 inches)
Weight: 7 to 10 kilograms (15 to 21 pounds)

The West Highland White Terrier has a double-layer coat that keeps it warm all year long. Tropical weather is often too much for this furry canine. The Westie is small yet sturdy. One might say these little dogs are strong from head to tail.

Personality: Although they are small, West Highland White Terriers are not lapdogs. They want to do what they please as much as possible.

Breed Background: Determined hunters, Westies have a long history of getting stuck in foxholes. Many owners have had to pull their dogs from these tight spaces – by their tails. Over time the breed has developed an amazingly solid tail.

Country of Origin: Scotland

Training Notes: Westies are smart and easy to train. However, these dogs should be kept on a lead or in a fenced garden because Westies will run after anything that moves.

Care Notes: To keep a Westie looking its best, daily brushing is important. Frequent baths are also recommended to keep its coat clean. Daily exercise is also necessary for this breed.

FUN FACT

The tips of a West Highland White Terrier's ears are prone to sunburn. Owners can prevent this problem by applying suntan lotion before heading outdoors with their pets.

Other terrier breeds

Australian Terrier ▶

Appearance:

Height: 20 to 26 centimetres (8 to 10 inches)
Weight: 6 to 7 kilograms (13 to 14 pounds)

Known for: being one of the quieter terriers
Country of Origin: Australia

Cesky Terrier

Appearance:

Height: 25 to 32 centimetres (10 to 13 inches)
Weight: 6 to 10 kilograms (13 to 22 pounds)

Known for: incredible stamina
Country of Origin: Czech Republic

Lakeland Terrier

Appearance:

Height: 34 to 37 centimetres (13 to 15 inches)
Weight: 7 to 8 kilograms (15 to 17 pounds)

Known for: wiry outer coat
Country of Origin: England

Norfolk Terrier ▶

Appearance:

Height: up to 25 centimetres (10 inches)

Weight: 5 to 6 kilograms (10 to 12 pounds)

Known for: fearlessness

Country of Origin: England

Sealyham Terrier ▼

Appearance:

Height: up to 30 centimetres (12 inches)

Weight: 8 to 9 kilograms (18 to 20 pounds)

Known for: calm nature

Country of Origin: Wales

Tiny toys

The Kennel Club's Toy group is made up of 23 dog breeds. These small breeds are noticeably different from most other groups. Many breeds were developed to assist their owners with fishing, herding or other work-related tasks. What toy group members have in common is their tiny, toy-like size.

Despite their size, these breeds are anything but **feeble**. Many toy group members are surprisingly active and energetic. These dogs enjoy a lot of the same activities as bigger breeds. Some owners enjoy carrying their tiny pets. But letting them walk – and run and play – gives them necessary exercise.

Toy group dogs can make excellent pets. Some people say their purpose is to be companions to their owners. These little dogs are ideal for people living in smaller spaces. Their small size also means lower costs and less work for owners. Nearly all supplies are cheaper for toy breeds. Exercising and cleaning up after these dogs also takes considerably less work and effort. What's not to love? Get ready for a close look at each breed!

FUN FACT

The Kennel Club also runs many dog activities and shows. These include Crufts and the International Agility Festival, the world's largest dog agility show.

Affenpinscher

FUN FACT

The word *affenpinscher* means "monkey terrier" in German.

FAMOUS DOGS

Artist Pierre-Auguste Renoir featured an Affenpinscher in his 1881 painting *Luncheon of the Boating Party*.

Appearance:
Height: 23 to 30 centimetres (9 to 12 inches)
Weight: 3 to 4 kilograms (6 to 9 pounds)

The Affenpinscher has a short, scruffy face. He has a rough, harsh-textured coat. His extended lower lip gives the breed a unique look. Many people think this dog looks like a tiny monkey.

Personality: Affenpinschers are known for their high energy levels. These playful dogs make fun family pets. They do best with older children, however, as younger children can hurt them too easily.

Breed Background: Affenpinschers are one of the oldest Toy dogs in Europe. They were developed as **ratters** during the 1600s. Ratters helped catch rats.

Countries of Origin: France, Germany

Training Notes: Like many Toy group members, this complex breed can be difficult to house-train. Beginning at a young age, crate training can make this task easier.

Care Notes: Affenpinschers need to be combed about twice per week to prevent mats. Their hair should look messy, so grooming this breed doesn't require much work.

Australian Silky Terrier

Appearance:

Height: 23 to 25 centimetres (9 to 10 inches)
Weight: 4 to 5 kilograms (8 to 10 pounds)

The Australian Silky Terrier has a long coat that parts down the middle. Its hair turns from black and tan to blue and tan over time.

Personality: The Silky Terrier has a bold yet playful personality. These dogs are curious, friendly and always on the move. They love people, but they're not the best choice for a home with pet rodents or reptiles.

Breed Background: One time known as the "Sydney Silky", Australian Silky Terriers were bred to hunt snakes.

Country of Origin: Australia

Training Notes: Silky Terriers are smart and trainable. But training may take more time with this stubborn breed. Positive praise and firm guidance is important for training Australian Silky Terriers.

Care Notes: Caring for this breed's long coat takes some effort. A daily brushing is necessary to prevent tangles. Australian Silky Terriers also need daily exercise to stay in shape.

FUN FACT

Australia gave a Silky Terrier called Fizo a Purple Cross, the nation's highest award for animal bravery. The dog saved four young children from a deadly Eastern Brown Snake.

Bichon Frise

FUN FACT

Many Bichons live between 14 and 16 years, making them one of the healthiest of all dog breeds.

Appearance:
Height: 23 to 30 centimetres (9 to 12 inches)
Weight: 5 to 7 kilograms (10 to 16 pounds)

Bichon Frises are small but sturdy. They have curly double coats. When they are clipped for a show, they have a round appearance. Their coats are typically white, but they may also have cream and apricot markings. Because they are hypoallergenic, they are popular pets for people with allergies.

Personality: Bichon Frises are devoted and entertaining companions. These lively dogs love being the centre of attention. Bichons are extroverts, full of confidence and intelligence. Some owners insist that these happy dogs actually smile.

Another good characteristic of Bichons is that they are not yappers. They have a happy temperament and are easy to live with. They need people to be happy. Bichons also get along well with other dogs and pets.

Breed Background: The Bichon Frise is of Mediterranean ancestry and is related to the Maltese. The breed is also known as the "Tenerife Dog" because sailors allegedly found them on that island in the 1300s, fell for their charms and took them back to France.

Area of Origin: Mediterranean

Training Notes: This intelligent breed can learn tricks quickly. Bichon Frises can take longer to house-train than other dogs. Bichons respond well to gentle, positive training.

Care Notes: The Bichon Frise's hair grows quickly. Owners must brush it often and trim it when it gets too long. These dogs have a lot of energy and need daily exercise, including walks. Dogs that do not get their daily exercise are more likely to develop behaviour problems.

FUN FACT

The Bichon Frise was a favourite in the French royal courts in the 1500s.

Bolognese

FUN FACT

Historically, the Bolognese breed was an acceptable gift in fashionable circles.

Appearance:
Height: 25 to 30 centimetres (10 to 12 inches)
Weight: 3 to 4 kilograms (5 to 9 pounds)

The Bolognese (*BOHL-oh-nays*) is a small, pure-white dog with a long and fluffy coat. Its hair is long all over its body, from head to tail. The Bolognese has a non-shedding, flocked coat.

Personality: The Bolognese is a smart and charming breed. It is slightly more reserved than its cousin, the Bichon Frise. The Bolognese can get along well with other animals if it is introduced to them at an early age.

Breed Background: This breed is closely related to the Bichon Frise and the Havanese. The Bolognese was developed during the Roman Era.

Country of Origin: Italy

Training Notes: Firm, guided training is important for Bolognese dogs. It may howl when its owner is busy, so it is important to give it rules and limits.

Care Notes: The Bolognese needs some regular exercise, including long walks. He delights in family activities. Regular grooming is necessary to keep it looking tidy.

Cavalier King Charles Spaniel

FUN FACT

The Cavalier King Charles Spaniel is one of the largest Toy group members.

Appearance:
Height: 30 to 33 centimetres (12 to 13 inches)
Weight: 6 to 8 kilograms (13 to 18 pounds)

Cavalier King Charles Spaniels come in four colours: black and tan, ruby, blenheim and tricolour. Blenheim dogs are the most common. They are chestnut, which is brown-red, and white. All Cavaliers have large, brown eyes that give the breed a gentle, melting expression.

Personality: The only thing more charming than the Cavalier's looks is its personality. This friendly dog loves everyone. It is one of the best Toy group breeds for families with children.

Breed Background: King Charles II gave this breed its name. The King loved these dogs so much that it was rarely seen without one.

Country of Origin: United Kingdom

Training Notes: Cavaliers are easy to train. This dog learns quickly and remembers commands well. He responds especially well to gentle obedience training.

Care Notes: Cavaliers need daily walks to fulfil their exercise needs. Daily brushing is also necessary to keep this breed looking its best.

Chihuahua (Smooth Coat)

FUN FACT

Some scientists think the Chihuahua descended from a wild animal called the fennec fox. This desert animal has large ears that look a lot like the Chihuahua's.

FAMOUS DOGS

The *Beverly Hills Chihuahua* films are about a spoiled and pampered Chihuahua called Chloe.

Appearance:
Height: 15 to 23 centimetres (6 to 9 inches)
Weight: 1 to 3 kilograms (2 to 6 pounds)

Chihuahuas are the smallest of all the Toy breeds. These brown-eyed, tiny canines come in several colours. Their hair may be short or long. Some dogs have small heads that are described as deer-shaped. Other Chihuahuas have bigger, round heads called apple-shaped.

Personality: Chihuahuas can make wonderful pets. They are highly affectionate animals. Most have one person in particular who becomes their favourite human. Usually this is the person who spends the most time with the dog.

Country of Origin: Mexico

Training Notes: This breed is smart and doesn't require a lot of training. When a Chihuahua is stubborn, it is important to keep training positive and upbeat.

Care Notes: Chihuahuas have a soft spot on the tops of their heads called a molera. Owners must be especially careful of their dogs' heads for this reason. Keeping these dogs on a healthy diet is also important. It doesn't take many extra calories to cause obesity in this breed.

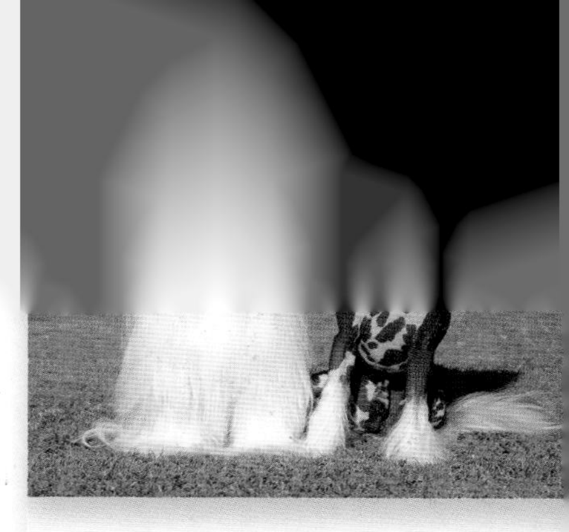

Appearance:

Height: 28 to 33 centimetres (11 to 13 inches)
Weight: up to 5 kilograms (12 pounds)

The Chinese Crested comes in two varieties: the Hairless and the Powder Puff. Several Chinese Cresteds have won ugly dog contests. Many dog enthusiasts think these dogs are beautiful, however. Their hairless bodies are topped with thick **plumes** of hair on their heads, feet and tails.

Personality: The Chinese Crested makes a great pet for a wide variety of people. These dogs bond closely with their human family members.

Areas of Origin: Africa, China

Training Notes: Some dog trainers insist that this breed is less intelligent than many others. This isn't the case. Cresteds simply have a different learning style than many other dogs. These stubborn dogs need more patience and a positive approach when it comes to training.

Care Notes: Owners must take special care of their Chinese Crested's exposed skin when heading outdoors. Sunscreen or a sweater is often necessary, depending on the weather. Just make sure that the sweater isn't made of wool. Many Chinese Cresteds are allergic to wool. Cresteds need less exercise than many other breeds. For this reason they can be a great match for the elderly or people who are disabled.

FUN FACT

Unlike most other dog breeds, Chinese Cresteds have sweat glands. For this reason they don't pant like other breeds.

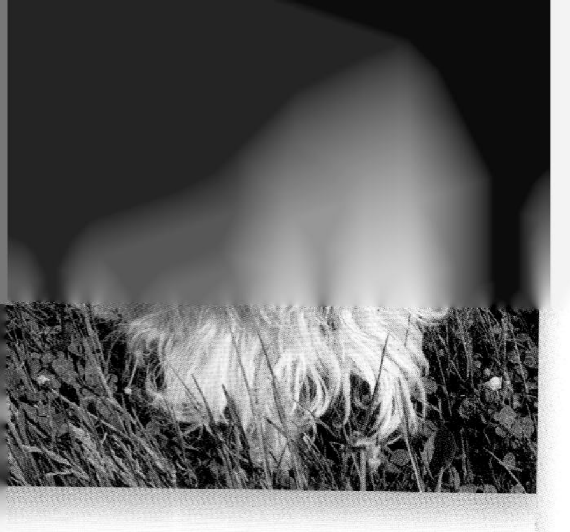

FUN FACT

The Coton de Tulear is related to the Bichon Frise and the Maltese.

Appearance:

Height: 20 to 30 centimetres (8 to 12 inches)
Weight: 4 to 7 kilograms (8 to 15 pounds)

The Coton De Tulear has a fluffy coat that looks like cotton. The Coton part of this breed's name means "cotton" in French. Its hair can be white, black and white, or tricolour.

Personality: Coton De Tulears can live almost anywhere. They make great pets and thrive on human companionship.

Breed Background: Some dog enthusiasts believe pirates brought this breed to the African city of Tulear. It is also known as the Royal Dog of Madagascar.

Country of Origin: Madagascar

Training Notes: These smart dogs learn quickly and love to please their owners. Some members of the breed even compete in agility. The Coton is a noisy dog and may bark often, so training should begin right away.

Care Notes: The Coton needs a fair amount of grooming. The fluffy coat tangles easily, so daily brushing is a must. It doesn't shed, however. Needing little exercise, this dog is happy with a short walk each day. Some Coton De Tulears enjoy swimming.

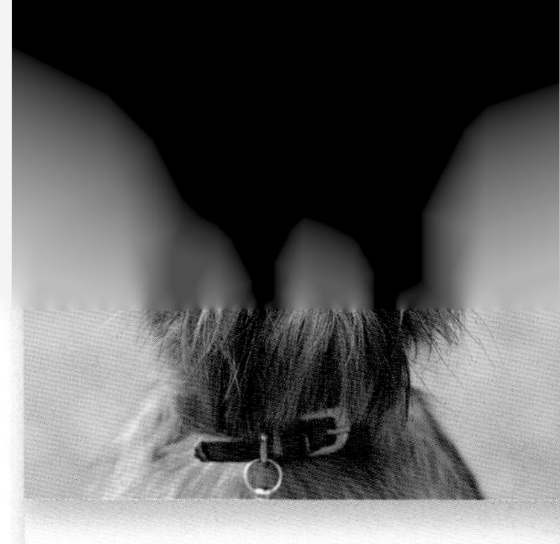

FUN FACT

Some people say this rough-coated breed looks like the Ewoks from the *Star Wars* films.

Appearance:
Height: 23 to 28 centimetres (9 to 11 inches)
Weight: 4 to 5 kilograms (8 to 10 pounds)

The Griffon Bruxellois has a short face and a square body. This breed may have a smooth or rough coat and is typically black, black and tan or red. Related to the Affenpinscher, the Griffon Bruxellois also has a monkey-like face.

Personality: These dogs have strong personalities. They can be lively, friendly and loving. They can also be grumpy, tense and demanding of their owners' attention. Many Griffons do not get along well with children.

Breed Background: The Griffon Bruxellois was developed in the 1600s in Belgium. They were used to rid barns of rodents.

Country of Origin: Belgium

Training Notes: Owners should start house-training a Griffon immediately. Staying on a schedule is also important. Still, accidents are common for this breed, even as adult dogs.

Care Notes: The Griffon Bruxellois needs regular exercise. A daily walk around the neighbourhood can be a good bonding experience with this dog. A Griffon needs regular feeding times. Griffon owners who leave food out all the time often end up with picky eaters.

FUN FACT

The Havanese is the national dog of Cuba. The breed is named after the nation's capital, Havana.

FAMOUS DOGS

Author Charles Dickens owned a Havanese named Tim.

Appearance:
Height: 23 to 28 centimetres (9 to 11 inches)
Weight: 3 to 6 kilograms (7 to 13 pounds)

The Havanese has long, wavy hair. This breed's coat is supposed to look a bit messy. The Havanese is known for its unique gait. The breed's front legs are slightly shorter than its back legs. This causes a noticeable spring to this animal's step.

Personality: The Havanese is a lively and affectionate breed. It enjoys being the centre of its family's attention. Unlike many Toy breeds, this dog doesn't bark a lot.

Breed Background: The Havanese's roots can be traced back to the Mediterranean during the 100s BC.

Country of Origin: Cuba

Training Notes: The Havanese is one of the easiest toy group members to house-train. These smart dogs enjoy pleasing their owners. Obedience training at an early age is also recommended for Havanese dogs.

Care Notes: The Havanese coat works a lot like a dust mop. Owners must brush their dogs several times each week. Havanese dogs that spend lots of time outdoors may need to be brushed even more frequently. Daily exercise is ideal for this breed.

Italian Greyhound

FUN FACT

Italian Greyhounds can run up to 40 kilometres (25 miles) per hour.

Appearance:
Height: 33 to 38 centimetres (13 to 15 inches)
Weight: 3 to 7 kilograms (7 to 15 pounds)

The Italian Greyound is a smaller version of the Greyhound. Similar to their bigger cousins, Italian Greyhounds are built for speed. Covered with smooth hair, their thin bodies are muscular.

Personality: Italian Greyhounds want to be with their owners as much as possible. These dogs are known for following their owners from room to room. They also love lying in the sun because it keeps these short-haired dogs warm.

Countries of Origin: Greece, Turkey

Training Notes: An Italian Greyhound can learn commands easily. But it is important to remember that this dog has a strong desire to hunt. It cannot be trusted off a lead, as this dog may chase a squirrel instead of obeying its owners. An Italian Greyhound can also be challenging to house-train.

Care Notes: An Italian Greyhound needs a coat if it will be outdoors in the winter. Some owners choose to train their dogs to use litter boxes during colder months. This breed can feel cold outdoors even on a rainy day in the summer. An Italian Greyhound loves to run and needs daily exercise.

FUN FACT

Japanese Chin are known for standing on their hind legs and spinning in a circle. Owners refer to this dance as the "Chin Spin".

Appearance:
Height: 20 to 28 centimetres (8 to 11 inches)
Weight: 2 to 4 kilograms (4 to 9 pounds)

People first notice the Japanese Chin's huge, round eyes. Set wide apart, they give the breed a unique expression. Its long, silky coat is single layered. The colours can be a combination of black, white, lemon and tan. It takes an adult dog about three years to grow a full coat.

Personality: Japanese Chin are loving, devoted dogs. They are also known for their intelligence and quiet nature. Unlike many toy group breeds, the Japanese Chin only barks occasionally.

Breed Background: This breed was developed as a lap breed for Asian nobility.

Countries of Origin: China, Japan

Training Notes: A Japanese Chin is easy to train. Starting at an early age is important. Socializing these dogs is the key to keeping them friendly.

Care Notes: This long-haired breed is surprisingly easy to groom. Brushing a Japanese Chin about twice a week is usually enough to keep its hair mat-free.

FUN FACT

The King Charles Spaniel was developed in the British Isles and is a favourite of British Royalty.

Appearance:
Height: 25 to 28 centimetres (10 to 11 inches)
Weight: 4 to 6 kilograms (8 to 14 pounds)

The King Charles Spaniel looks a lot like the Cavalier King Charles Spaniel. The two breeds are closely related. The King Charles Spaniel has several unique features. First, it is slightly smaller. The King Charles also has a flatter face, pushed-back nose and a dome-shaped head.

Personality: King Charles Spaniels are known for being quieter than Cavaliers. They also take longer to warm up to new people. Once they have bonded, however, they are every bit as loving as their Cavalier cousins. Most King Charles Spaniels also get along well with other dogs and cats.

Country of Origin: England

Training Notes: This is an independent breed. Training a King Charles Spaniel isn't difficult. It does take a determined trainer, however. Charlies often try to ignore commands they do not want to follow.

Care Notes: King Charles Spaniels are easy to groom but require regular brushing. Combing through the long hair on its ears also prevents matting. The breed also needs a daily walk or a good romp in a fenced-in garden.

Löwchen (Little Lion Dog)

FUN FACT

It's no surprise that this dog's hairstyle is called a lion cut. The name *Löwchen* means "lion" in German.

Appearance:
Height: 30 to 36 centimetres (12 to 14 inches)
Weight: 4 to 8 kilograms (9 to 18 pounds)

The Löwchen's distinctive haircut is short on the rump, legs and tail. Each leg has a furry cuff of fur above the foot. The tail has a large plume on the end. These dogs come in up to 18 different colour variations, including black, black and silver and chocolate.

Personality: The Löwchen is a gentle, playful breed. It is an affectionate companion to its human family members. Löwchen can be a bit shy with strangers. They warm up quickly to other animals, however.

Country of Origin: Germany

Training Notes: Löwchen bark a lot and will alert their owners to whatever might be going on near by. They can make good watchdogs for this reason. Owners must train these dogs so they don't bark excessively.

Care Notes: The Löwchen coat doesn't require a great deal of care. Some brushing is necessary to keep the hair from matting. Because of its high energy level, the Löwchen enjoys daily exercise, including walks.

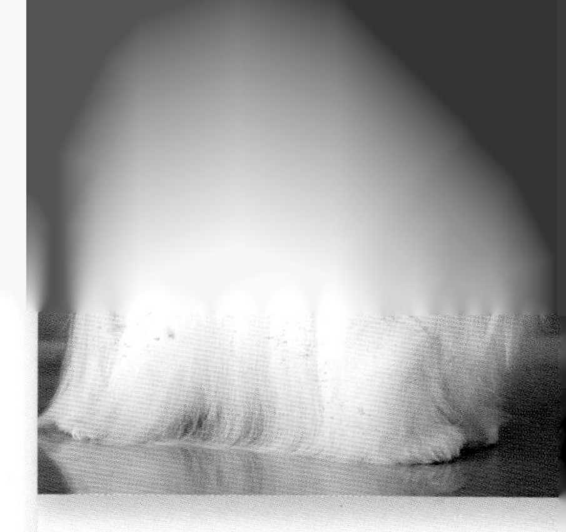

Appearance:
Height: 20 to 25 centimetres (8 to 10 inches)
Weight: 2 to 3 kilograms (4 to 6 pounds)

The Maltese has silky, white hair. When kept long and groomed for a show, its hair hangs flat, almost touching the ground. Its big, dark eyes and black nose are its trademarks. Its body is small but sturdy.

FUN FACT

Long ago, the Greeks built special tombs for their Maltese pets.

Personality: The Maltese is one of the sweetest toy breeds. This breed is known for being affectionate with its owners. These dogs love to sit on family members' laps. Many Maltese even ride in bags carried by their owners.

Breed Background: The Maltese is one of the oldest dog breeds. Ancient Egyptians are said to have worshipped these tiny dogs. The breed's name, however, comes from the island of Malta – where the breed was developed.

Country of Origin: Malta

Training Notes: Maltese can learn basic commands easily. A Maltese that has been spoiled too much can sometimes resist training. It can also take this breed a little more time to catch on to house-training.

Care Notes: A Maltese's long, white coat is hard to keep clean and free of tangles. Owners should brush these dogs daily. Baths are necessary about once a week. Despite their size, this breed is surprisingly athletic. Maltese love to run around and play.

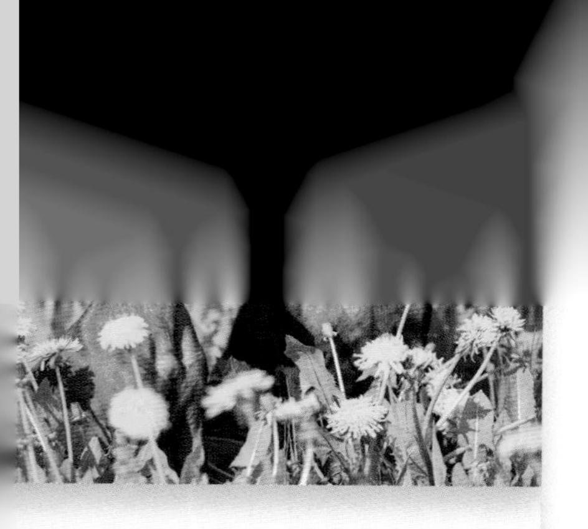

FUN FACT

The Miniature Pinscher is especially popular in Scandinavia.

Appearance:
Height: 25 to 30 centimetres (10 to 12 inches)
Weight: 4 to 5 kilograms (8 to 10 pounds)

The Miniature Pinscher has a confusing name. This breed is not a smaller version of the Doberman Pinscher. It is its own separate breed. The Min Pin comes in several colours. These include red, black and red-brown, and chocolate and red-brown.

Personality: Miniature Pinschers have a lot of confidence. Nicknamed the "King of Toys", this little dog doesn't see itself as small. The Min Pin is curious, fearless and full of energy. These dogs can make great pets for people who can keep up with them.

Breed Background: The Miniature Pinscher was developed by crossing a Dachshund, Italian Greyhound and the short-haired German Pinscher. It was used as a barn ratter.

Country of Origin: Germany

Training Notes: Min Pins are trainable with persistence and patience. Obedience training should begin at a young age, and training should be done within a fenced area. These dogs love to chase anything that catches their attention.

Care Notes: Min Pins need a tremendous amount of exercise for such little dogs. Still, owners should avoid jumping activities. The breed's brittle bones can break easily. It should be brushed only when needed.

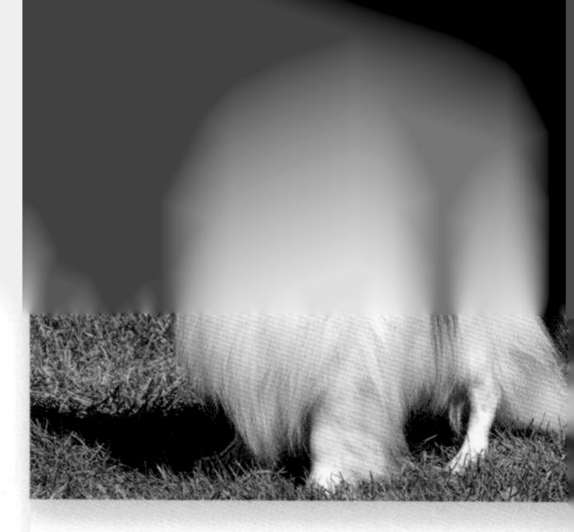

Appearance:

Height: 20 to 28 centimetres (8 to 11 inches)
Weight: 3 to 5 kilograms (7 to 10 pounds)

The Papillon is one of the easiest toy group members to recognise. Its large, upright ears are covered with fur. Many people think the ears look like butterflies. Papillons have long, silky hair. Their coats are always white with patches of another colour.

Personality: These tiny dogs have an incredible energy level. They can be excellent pets for families with older children. The breed is known to snap at small children, however.

Countries of Origin:

France, Belgium

Training Notes: This breed is highly intelligent and trainable. Owners should make sure to socialize their Papillons. These little dogs can end up aggressive if they aren't introduced to people and other pets at a young age. House-training this breed can take some extra time and effort.

Care Notes: Papillons need daily exercise time. These dogs are fairly easy to groom. Despite their long coats, brushing is only necessary about once per week.

FUN FACT

In the French language, ***papillon*** means "butterfly".

Pekingese

FUN FACT

At one time only royals were allowed to own a Pekingese. Stealing one of these dogs was punishable by death.

Appearance:

Height: 15 to 23 centimetres (6 to 9 inches)
Weight: under 6 kilograms (14 pounds)

An old story states that the Pekingese was born after a lion fell in love with a monkey. This hairy little dog looks like both animals. They have flat faces and large, round eyes. These features can be hard to see sometimes under the breed's heavy double coat.

A Pekingese can be any colour, with the exception of albino or liver. Some Pekingese have a black face too. The outer coat is long and course in texture. The undercoat is soft and thick.

Personality: Pekingese are bold and fear nothing. At the same time, they are among the most affectionate breeds. They enjoy sitting on their owners' laps and being petted. Pekingese do not usually get along well with children, however.

This breed makes a good watchdog because they are often wary of strangers. Behavioural problems commonly associated with Pekingese include growling, snapping or biting. With proper training, these issues can be eliminated.

Breed Background: The Pekingese gets its name from the ancient Chinese city of Peking, which is now Beijing. Emperors of China used these tiny yet courageous animals as guard dogs. When an Emperor died, his Pekingese was also sacrificed so the dog could join him in the afterlife.

Country of Origin: China

Training Notes: Training a Pekingese can be difficult. They are stubborn. This breed also prefers an indoor potty spot instead of going outside. Positive rewards, such as praise and treats, may help train a Pekingese.

Care Notes: Grooming a Pekingese is a lot of work. They need to be brushed daily and bathed often. Their eyes and skin also need to be wiped clean regularly. Although he likes to exercise, a Pekingese is not fussy. An occasional walk with its owner is enough to keep it happy.

FUN FACT

Pekingese are sometimes called Peking Palasthunds.

FUN FACT

Pomeranians descend from sled dogs of Finland and Iceland. Alaskan Malamutes, Samoyeds, Siberian Huskies and Keeshonds are among the Pomeranian's ancestors.

Appearance:
Height: 18 to 30 centimetres (7 to 12 inches)
Weight: 1 to 3 kilograms (3 to 7 pounds)

The Pomeranian's double coat is long and fluffy. The hair around the dog's neck is longer than the rest of its coat. This fur is called the frill. Pomeranians come in a wide variety of colours. Red, orange, brown and black dogs are the most common.

Personality: Pomeranians are bold and intelligent dogs. Some have been known to boss around much larger breeds. Alert and curious, Poms definitely have minds of their own.

Breed Background: When this breed was developed, Pomeranians weighed up to seven times more than today's dogs. England's Queen Victoria began breeding smaller dogs to create Pomeranians that could be lapdogs. Their name, however, comes from a German province called Pomerania.

Countries of Origin: Poland, Germany

Training Notes: Poms are easy to train if owners begin working on the task early. This breed is smart but stubborn. Poms that lack stimulation often bark to the point of becoming an annoyance to neighbours.

Care Notes: Many of these little dogs are hardy athletes. These Poms may show off their talents in agility or flyball. These canine sports can help provide the breed with the exercise it needs. Weekly grooming, including brushing and bathing, is recommended for Poms.

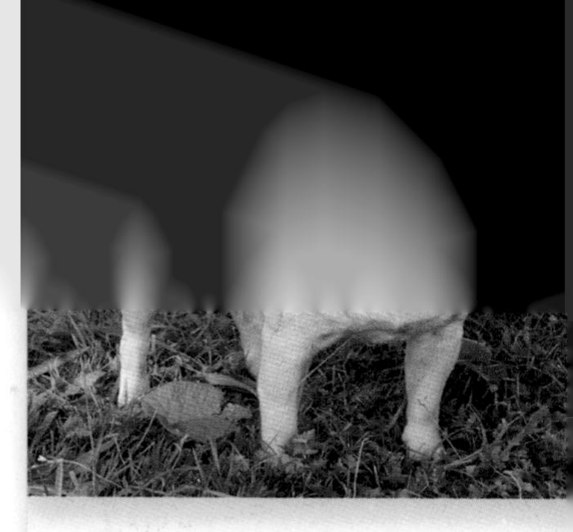

FUN FACT

A Pug saved the life of the Netherlands' Prince William of Orange in 1572. The little dog warned its master that the Spaniards were on their way to attack him. The royal soon named the Pug the official dog of the House of Orange.

Appearance:
Height: 30 to 36 centimetres (12 to 14 inches)
Weight: 6 to 8 kilograms (14 to 18 pounds)

Most Pugs have short double coats. Many members of this breed are fawn, or yellow-brown. This tan colour comes in several shades, such as apricot, or yellow-orange and silver. Other dogs are black. All Pugs have black muzzles. This breed's flat face is covered with wrinkles.

Personality: Pugs have one of the best temperaments out of all the breeds in the toy group. They get along with children exceptionally well and make great family pets. The breed isn't very active, however. Children who want to play ball or fetch may prefer another breed.

Country of Origin: China

Training Notes: Pugs are smart and trainable. Owners will have the best results using food rewards.

Care Notes: A Pug's wrinkles trap a lot of moisture. Owners should clean the face daily to prevent skin infections. The Pug's flat face makes it hard for the dog to breathe in warm weather. Some dogs even require surgery to correct this problem.

FUN FACT

The Yorkshire Terrier is one of the most recognizable dog breeds out of any breed group.

Appearance:

Height: 18 to 23 centimetres (7 to 9 inches)
Weight: 1 to 3 kilograms (3 to 7 pounds)

The Yorkshire Terrier is born with a black and tan coat. As the puppy grows, the black turns into a blue-grey colour. The breed's coat is naturally long.

The Yorkie's coat consists of hair, not fur. For this important reason, the breed is often an option for people who are allergic to other dogs. Hair holds far less **dander** than fur. Some people are allergic to dander.

Personality: Yorkies make great pets for adults and families with older children. Younger children must be taught to treat these small dogs with respect. Yorkies tend to snap at people if they feel threatened.

Breed Background: The Yorkshire Terrier was developed in northern England. The Yorkie's ancestors include the Skye Terrier, Dandie Dinmont, Manchester Terrier, Maltese and one breed that is now extinct – the Clydesdale Terrier. These early breed members worked as rat hunters for the working class. Many Yorkies worked in the cellars of factories. Soon after, however, higher classes discovered the breed. He later became a popular pet for high society members.

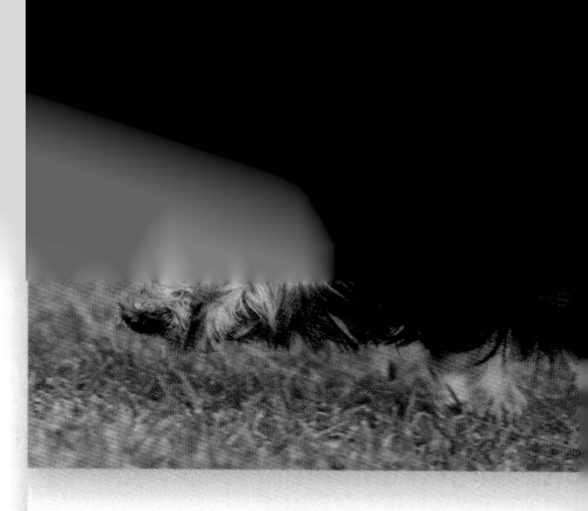

Country of Origin: England

Training Notes: Yorkies are highly in tune with their owners and can be trained easily. Getting them to pay attention is easy. They learn commands quickly and love praise.

Care Notes: These small dogs have a great amount of energy and love to run around inside or outdoors. A daily walk can help prevent behavioural problems from developing if this dog gets too bored.

A Yorkie's silky coat needs daily brushing and weekly baths. Shorter coats can be maintained with weekly brushing and only occasional bathing.

FUN FACT

Most dogs lose their baby teeth naturally. Yorkies, though, sometimes need a trip to the vet to help with this process. If a new tooth is trying to come in but can't, it can cause the adult tooth to come in crooked.

FUN FACT

Some of the breeds in the Utility group are among the oldest documented dog breeds in the world, including the Shar Pei, the Chow Chow and the Shih Tzu.

Diverse dogs

The Kennel Club's Utility group is made up of 30 dog breeds. Dogs in the utility group are all different. These dogs vary in size, coat type and personality. One breed doesn't even have hair! While each breed is different, they all have one thing in common – they are not used as sporting or working animals.

Some utility breeds are wildly popular, such as the Poodle. Others are extremely rare, such as the Tibetan Spaniel. Dalmatians are large, while other dogs are much smaller, such as the Kooikerhondje. A couple of breeds – the Bulldog and French Bulldog – are known for having wrinkly foreheads. One breed, the Shar Pei, has wrinkles all over.

The utility group is one of the most varied of all seven Kennel Club groups. These fascinating animals come from more than a dozen different nations. Some have been recognized by the Kennel Club for more than 100 years. Others have been recognised more recently. Get ready for a close look at each breed!

Akita

FUN FACT

Helen Keller, an American author and political activist, brought the first Akita to the United States in 1937. She discovered the breed on a trip to Japan. Keller was the first deaf and blind person to earn a Bachelor of Arts degree.

Appearance:
Height: 61 to 71 centimetres (24 to 28 inches)
Weight: 29 to 52 kilograms (65 to 115 pounds)

Akitas are known for their sturdy bodies and curled tails. Members of this breed have thick, heavy fur. Akitas can be any colour variety, including white brindle or pinto. Brindle is a **tawny**, streaked colour, and pinto means having patches of white or another colour.

Personality: Akitas are sometimes bold and aggressive with other dogs. They tend to show dominance. However they love their human family members with great intensity and loyalty. They are protective towards their owners.

Breed Background: The Akita Inu, meaning "large dog", originated many centuries ago in the ancient polar regions of Japan. The Akita was originally developed as a fighting dog but was converted into a hunting dog. Akitas hunted large game, such as black bear, deer and wild boar.

Country of Origin: Japan

Training Notes: Akitas are intelligent but stubborn. Without training they can become even more aggressive around other animals. Training should be consistent from a young age for Akitas.

Care Notes: All Akitas need regular exercise. A long, daily walk is ideal. Their coats also need regular brushing and bathing to prevent excessive shedding.

FUN FACT

The Akita is the national dog of Japan.

Boston Terrier

FUN FACT

The Boston Terrier is nicknamed the "American Gentleman" for its personality and appearance. Some people think this charming dog's dark and white coat pattern looks like a **tuxedo**.

Appearance:
Height: 38 to 43 centimetres (15 to 17 inches)
Weight: not exceeding 11.5 kilograms (25 pounds)

Many Boston terriers have a black and white colour pattern that helps them stand out from other dog breeds. Others are black brindle and white, brindle and white, or seal brindle and white. Boston Terriers are also known for their large eyes and **expressive** faces.

Personality: Boston Terriers are alert, intelligent and kind. They love people. Boston Terriers are known for their big hearts and clownish ways. They don't bark as much as many other terriers. They do, however, have a few unpleasant habits. The breed is known for grunting, snoring and passing gas.

Country of Origin: United States

Training Notes: Boston Terriers are smart but sensitive. An owner's harsh tone can delay training progress. These dogs also tend to be stubborn. Owners should be persistent yet positive whenever working with this breed.

Care Notes: Nearly all dogs love food. But Boston Terriers seem to enjoy eating even more than other dogs. Owners must watch how much they feed their Boston Terriers for this reason. Many members of this breed end up overweight, which can cause health problems. Boston Terriers enjoy daily walks. An occasional bath and brushing also keep this dog's coat looking its best.

Bulldog

Appearance:

Height: 30 to 41 centimetres (12 to 16 inches)
Weight: 23 to 25 kilograms (50 to 55 pounds)

Bulldogs have large heads, heavy bodies and short, **bowed** legs. Common Bulldog coat colours are brindle, white and various shades of red or fawn.

Personality: Members of this breed are alert, loyal and dependable. A Bulldog also gets along well with new people and with children as long as the dog is socialized when it is young.

Country of Origin: United Kingdom

Training Notes: Bulldogs can be stubborn and lazy. This breed often needs to be convinced to go for a walk. Because of their stubbornness, Bulldogs can also take longer to house-train than other dog breeds. Training should begin early and include treats and praise as rewards.

Care Notes: A Bulldog's wrinkles need to be wiped clean with a damp cloth regularly. Even more importantly owners must be extra careful with this breed near water. Unlike most dogs, Bulldogs are not naturally good at swimming.

FUN FACT

The Bulldog is the national dog of the United Kingdom and is associated throughout the world with the legendary John Bull, a cartoon character that represented the United Kingdom, especially England.

FAMOUS DOGS

This breed is a symbol of some impressive institutions. A Bulldog is the official **mascot** of Churchill College, Cambridge and Bath Spa University, Somerset.

Canaan Dog

FUN FACT

The Canaan Dog was the first breed used to sniff for land mines in ancient war regions.

Appearance:
Height: 50 to 60 centimetres (20 to 24 inches)
Weight: 18 to 25 kilograms (40 to 55 pounds)

The Canaan Dog has a square-shaped body. The Canaan's double coat is short but protective. Its coat keeps it warm in the winter and cool in the summer. This breed is typically sand-coloured, red-brown, white, black or spotted.

Personality: Canaans are naturally curious. They love exploring. Canaans also bond closely with their human family members. These dogs are also alert and serve as effective guard dogs.

Breed Background: Nomadic desert people in the Middle East developed this rare breed. *Canaan* is the ancient name for Israel.

Country of Origin: Israel

Training Notes: This breed can be easy to train if obedience training and socialization begins early. Otherwise a Canaan might try to dominate its owner.

Care Notes: Canaans need plenty of space and exercise. The short coat makes this dog easy to groom. Because it is a seasonal shedder, some brushing is necessary on a weekly basis.

Chow Chow

Appearance:

Height: 46 to 56 centimetres (1 to 22 inches)
Weight: 20 to 36 kilograms (45 to 80 pounds)

With its large **ruff**, the Chow Chow looks like a small lion. Its coat can be rough or smooth and comes in a variety of colours – red, black, blue, fawn, white and cream.

Personality: Although it looks cuddly, this breed is not known for its friendly nature. Chow Chows take time to bond with people. Once they do, however, they are fiercely loyal. They sometimes can act aggressively towards children, strangers and other pets.

Breed Background: Chinese emperors used this breed for hunting, guarding and pulling sleds.

Country of Origin: China

Training Notes: A Chow Chow can be stubborn. For this reason the breed needs early obedience training and socialization.

Care Notes: Chow Chows enjoy daily exercise. An inactive Chow Chow is likely to be irritable. They also need regular bathing and daily brushing to keep their thick coats in good condition.

FUN FACT

Chow Chows have a bluish-black tongue.

FAMOUS DOGS

Author Vanna Bonta owns a red Chow Chow named Beowulf. He appears in the book *Flight*, written by Bonta.

Dalmatian

FUN FACT

The Dalmatian is also known as the Carriage Dog, English Coach Dog and the Plum Pudding Dog.

FAMOUS DOGS

Disney has made two films called *101 Dalmatians*. The first was a cartoon, while the second featured live animals. Both films follow the adventures of two Dalmatians named Pongo and Perdita.

Appearance:
Height: 56 to 61 centimetres (22 to 24 inches)
Weight: 20 to 32 kilograms (45 to 70 pounds)

The Dalmatian is one of the most recognizable breeds in the world. It is known for its spotted coat. Some Dalmatians have only a few spots. Others are covered from head to tail in black markings. Many Dalmatians even have spots on the inside of their mouths.

Personality: Dalmatians can make great pets. They get along well with older children. When happy, these lively dogs are even known to curl their lips into a smile.

Country of Origin: Dalmatia (present-day Croatia)

Training Notes: Dalmatians are smart dogs and easily trained. They cannot be trusted off lead, however. This independent breed is known for its tendency to run away whenever it gets the chance. These dogs often excel in competitive sports, such as agility and rally events.

Care Notes: Its short coat doesn't mat. It does shed, though. Regular brushing can help remove dead hair. This short-haired breed needs a coat or sweater in colder climates. They need a lot of exercise, such as daily running or walking.

Eurasier

FUN FACT

The Eurasier is also known as the Wolfspitz.

Appearance:
Height: 48 to 60 centimetres (19 to 24 inches)
Weight: 18 to 32 kilograms (40 to 70 pounds)

The Eurasier has a harsh, thick double coat. Its fur is shorter on its muzzle, ears, face and front legs. This dog can be of any colour variety except all-white.

Personality: The Eurasier is a devoted companion and bonds strongly with its family. It is calm and gentle and a vigilant watchdog. However, it can be reserved with strangers.

Breed Background: Although this breed was developed recently, it is believed that the Eurasier is regenerated from the ancient Russian breed, the Laika.

Country of Origin: Germany

Training Notes: The Eurasier is easy to train and eager to please its owner. Obedience training should begin at an early age.

Care Notes: The Eurasier's coat must be regularly groomed, as he sheds at least once per year. This dog also enjoys walks, several times per day. Hiking, swimming or playing fetch are also good outlets for expending energy.

FUN FACT

Contrary to its name, the French Bulldog isn't French. English people brought this breed to France when they moved there from Nottingham.

French Bulldog

Appearance:
Height: up to 30 centimetres (12 inches)
Weight: 11 to 13 kilograms (24 to 28 pounds)

French Bulldogs are sturdy dogs. They have large, square heads and rounded foreheads. The skin is loose, forming wrinkles around the head and shoulders. Their bat-like ears and flat faces add to their distinctive look.

French Bulldogs come in several colours. Sometimes called Frenchies, these small dogs may be brindle, fawn or pied. They can also be a mix of these colours. Pied means having two or more different colours, such as a combination of brindle and fawn.

Personality: French Bulldogs make great pets. They are playful, alert and affectionate. They're not loud dogs, but they love to clown around. The Frenchie gets along well with strangers and plays well with other dogs.

Breed Background: French Bulldogs originated in the 1800s in Nottingham. They were created by crossing small Bulldogs with Pugs and Terriers. Lace makers wanted a smaller, lap version of the Bulldog. In the 1860s the Industrial Revolution brought craftspeople to France, and they took their dogs with them. This is where they were given their name.

Country of Origin: England

Training Notes: Frenchies strive to please their owners and can be trained easily with positive motivation, such as treats. Socialization with other animals and people should start right away.

Care Notes: French Bulldogs need a daily walk. They love to run and play for hours. However, their short muzzles can get in the way of warm weather fun. Breathing can be difficult for this breed, especially when the weather is hot.

Frenchies need their wrinkles cleaned regularly. Grooming their short coats is easy. An occasional bath is all that is needed.

FUN FACT

Believe it or not, the French Bulldog loves to hunt mice.

German Spitz (Klein)

FUN FACT

The tiniest versions of the German Spitz (Klein) breed weigh in at only 2.3 kilograms (5 pounds).

Appearance:

Height: 23 to 29 centimetres (9 to 12 inches)
Weight: 5 to 18 kilograms (11 to 40 pounds)

The German Spitz comes in two varieties: Klein, the smaller of the two, and Mittel. The two are identical in shape and characteristics. The German Spitz has a distinct curly tail and a soft, long coat, coming in any colour variation.

Personality: The German Spitz is independent and known for having a happy outlook on life. It makes an ideal pet because it can get along well with anyone, young and old.

Breed Background: In Europe, Spitz dogs were associated with the hunter-gatherers of the first Stone Age. The German Spitz hails from the Northern German plain that stretches from the Rhine to Vistula.

Country of Origin: Germany

Training Notes: Because the German Spitz breed is a good watchdog, it should be trained at an early age how to behave properly in regards to barking and meeting new people. Firm training works best with this breed, or it might become too demanding with its owner.

Care Notes: Regular brushing is needed for this dog's long coat in order to prevent matting. The German Spitz, both varieties, should be exercised daily.

Japanese Shiba Inu

Appearance:
Height: 37 to 40 centimetres (15 to 16 inches)
Weight: 8 to 10 kilograms (17 to 23 pounds)

The Shiba Inu's pointed ears and reddish colouring make the breed look like a small fox. This breed has a short yet thick coat. The dense fur actually repels dirt, making the Shiba Inu one of the cleanest dog breeds.

FUN FACT

The Shiba Inu is one of the most popular pet dogs in Japan.

Personality: The Shiba Inu is loyal and loving. Because the breed is independent, some people see the breed as unfriendly. Many owners compare the Shiba Inu's personality with that of a cat. They love their owners – on their own terms.

Breed Background: This ancient breed was developed to hunt birds, bears and boar in the mountainous regions of Japan.

Country of Origin: Japan

Training Notes: This breed is known for being one of the toughest dogs to train. Early puppy socialization and obedience classes are needed for these strong-willed dogs.

Care Notes: Another reason people liken Shiba Inu to cats is that these dogs are fussy about their appearance. They constantly self-groom. Owners still have to brush these dogs to keep shedding to a minimum.

Keeshond

FUN FACT

Known as the Dutch Barge Dog, the Keeshond is the national dog of the Netherlands.

Appearance:

Height: 43 to 46 centimetres (17 to 18 inches)
Weight: 23 to 29 kilograms (50 to 65 pounds)

Keeshonden look a lot like teddy bears. Their double coats are tricoloured. Their hair is a mix of black, cream and grey. They have characteristics of Spitz breeds, including a curly tail and alert, pointed ears. This breed bears a strong resemblance to its ancestor, the Samoyed.

Personality: Keeshonden love people. Great with children, these dogs make excellent family pets. They love to be a part of the family and to be included in activities. Keeshonden tend to bark a lot, though, especially when meeting visitors.

Breed Background: The Keeshond descends from the Samoyed, the Chow Chow, the Finnish Spitz, the Norwegian Elkhound and the Pomeranian. It is an arctic dog. At the beginning of the French Revolution (1789–1799), the Keeshond was a symbol of the Dutch Patriot political party. Later when the Keeshond was brought to the USA, it became known as the Dutch Barge Dog. Keeshonden worked as watchdogs and guard dogs on riverboats, barges and on farms.

Country of Origin: Netherlands

Training Notes: Keeshonden enjoy pleasing their owners. They are also smart, so training them is easy. Basic obedience training should begin early on so that good habits are learned right away.

Care Notes: Keeshonden love to explore, so daily walks are recommended. They also love a good romp in an open, safe field. When a Keeshond spins in circles, it is a sign that it needs more exericse and stimulation.

This fluffy breed needs to be groomed twice per week, including brushing out dead hair. Bathe or dry shampoo only when necessary.

FUN FACT

The Keeshond is sometimes also called the Wolfspitz or the German Wolfspitz.

FUN FACT

The Kooikerhondje's eye-catching coat is used by duck hunters to attract swimming ducks into netting traps.

Kooikerhondje

Appearance:
Height: 35 to 42 centimetres (14 to 17 inches)
Weight: 9 to 18 kilograms (20 to 40 pounds)

The Kooikerhondje (*KOY-ker-hond*) has a medium-length coat that is slightly wavy. This dog is white with patches of orange-red fur. It also has black-tipped ears. It can take up to two years for this dog's distinctive coat to fully mature.

Personality: The Kooikerhondje's affectionate and friendly nature makes it a great family pet. It can be cautious around other dogs and strangers, but it doesn't take long for it to become accustomed to somebody.

Country of Origin: Netherlands

Training Notes: Kooikerhondjes are known for excessive chewing and occasional biting. These dogs need consistent and firm training before behavioural problems develop. However, these dogs do not respond well to a loud voice, so use positive praise and treats instead.

Care Notes: The Kooikerhondje's coat is not difficult to care for. It needs regular brushing and bathing to keep its shedding under control though. It also loves to be outdoors and needs daily exercise to keep it happy.

Lhasa Apso

FUN FACT

The oldest known Lhasa Apso lived to the age of 29!

Appearance:
Height: 23 to 28 centimetres (9 to 11 inches)
Weight: 5 to 8 kilograms (12 to 18 pounds)

The Lhasa Apso has a long double coat. Some owners keep their Lhasa Apso's hair short to make the hair easier to groom. The coat comes in a variety of colours, including gold, black, slate, white or brown.

Personality: Lhasa Apsos are loyal dogs and adore their human family members. Some people describe Lhasas as clownish and silly. This small breed can be afraid of strangers, though.

Breed Background: The Lhasa Apso originated in the Himalayan Mountains hundreds of years ago. The breed is named after the sacred city of Lhasa in Tibet, China.

Country of Origin: Tibet

Training Notes: Llasas can be stubborn, so positive and motivational training is key. Early socialization with other animals and people is important for these dogs too.

Care Notes: Lhasas need a lot of grooming to avoid matting. Weekly brushing is necessary. These dogs also enjoy regular, long walks each day.

Mexican Hairless

FUN FACT

About one in every five Mexican Hairless puppies is born with a full coat of short hair.

FAMOUS DOGS

The Mexican Hairless breed appears in many paintings by the Mexican artists Frida Kahlo and Diego Rivera.

Appearance:
Height: 46 to 60 centimetres (18 to 24 inches)
Weight: 11 to 18 kilograms (25 to 40 pounds)

Despite its name, this breed isn't completely hairless. It does have a small amount of hair on its back, tail and the top of its head. Also known as the Xoloitzcuintli (*show-low-itz-KWEENT-lee*), the Mexican Hairless stands out from other breeds mostly for its looks.

Personality: Called the "Xolo" for short, this breed can make a great pet. These dogs get along well with children. Mexican Hairless dogs are also known for their intelligence, loyalty and extreme devotion to their human family members.

Breed Background: The Mexican Hairless is one of the oldest dog breeds in the world. Because this breed is naturally warm, ancient Aztec people slept with the dog closeby to stay warm.

Country of Origin: Mexico

Training Notes: The Mexican Hairless needs consistent training and lots of praise. Regular socialization with other animals should be maintained throughout its life.

Care Notes: Unlike other breeds, the Mexican Hairless doesn't require brushing. Instead, its owners must care for its skin. This breed is prone to acne and other skin conditions. Keeping its skin clean and moisturized helps prevent these problems.

Miniature Schnauzer

FUN FACT

The Miniature Schnauzer was the earliest recognised breed among the three Schnauzer breeds.

Appearance:

Height: 33 to 36 centimetres (13 to 14 inches)
Weight: 6 to 7 kilograms (13 to 15 pounds)

The Miniature Schnauzer has a wiry coat. Its coat can be solid black, salt and pepper or black and silver. These dogs also have bushy whiskers and eyebrows.

Personality: A Miniature Schnauzer loves its human family members dearly. It loves to be a companion. An excellent watchdog, this breed will bark to alert its owners of approaching strangers.

Country of Origin: Germany

Training Notes: Trainers rank the Miniature Schnauzer among the smartest dog breeds. They are capable of learning complex commands. They also have incredible enthusiasm for learning new things.

Care Notes: Caring for a Miniature Schnauzer involves a lot of time. This dog's coat, including its famous moustache, needs daily brushing. A Mini Schnauzer also needs room to run, so a fenced garden is ideal for this breed.

Poodle

FUN FACT

Some Poodles have been crossed with other breeds to make other allergy-friendly breeds. A Cockapoo was created by crossing a Poodle with the Cocker Spaniel. A Labradoodle is part Poodle and part Labrador Retriever.

Appearance:

Toy
Height: under 28 centimetres (11 inches)
Weight: 3 to 4 kilograms (6 to 9 pounds)

Miniature
Height: 28 to 38 centimetres (11 to 15 inches)
Weight: 7 to 8 kilograms (15 to 17 pounds)

Standard
Height: over 38 centimetres (15 inches)
Weight: 20 to 32 kilograms (45 to 70 pounds)

The Poodle comes in three different sizes: Toy, Miniature and Standard. These curly canines come in many colours. Black, brown and white Poodles are the most common. If Poodles are groomed traditionally, their haircuts are easy to spot. Their coats include large puffs of hair as well as shaved areas. Many pet Poodle owners trim their dogs' coats more evenly.

Personality: Poodles are popular pets – and for good reason. These smart, lively dogs are a lot of fun to have around. Poodles are incredibly loyal and loving. Poodles are clowns by nature, providing plenty of amusement for their owners. Protective of their families, Poodles also make great guard dogs.

Breed Background: The word *Poodle* comes from a German word meaning "puddle". This is fitting because the breed began as a water retriever in the marshes of Germany.

FUN FACT

Over time the Poodle's hair will cord naturally if it isn't trimmed. The cords look like dreadlocks.

Country of Origin: Germany

Training Notes: Poodles are regularly ranked among the most intelligent dog breeds. Despite this fact they still need training to make pleasant pets. Socialization should begin at an early age in this dog's life. Without proper rules reinforced, Poodles tend to bark a lot too.

The biggest mistake a Poodle owner can make is thinking that these dogs naturally know how to behave properly. A bored Poodle can get into a lot of trouble!

Care Notes: This breed's hair doesn't shed like many other breeds. For this reason Poodles are a great choice for people who are allergic to the dander found on many dogs. Owners who want to keep their Poodles looking like show dogs must be prepared to groom them a lot. Some owners rely on a professional groomer for this important task. This breed's fast-growing coat can make these appointments frequent and expensive.

The Poodle is an active breed that needs daily exercise. It excels at hunting and agility events, if properly trained.

Schipperke

FUN FACT

The Schipperke can be credited with the first one-breed dog show in 1690.

Appearance:
Height: 25 to 33 centimetres (10 to 13 inches)
Weight: 5 to 8 kilograms (12 to 16 pounds)

The Schipperke is a small, black dog with pointed ears. Although most Schipperkes are black, some can also be fawn or cream. The short double coat is longer behind the dog's ears and around its neck.

Personality: This breed is known for its mischievous ways. A Schipperke seems to have no idea how little it is. It is aloof with strangers but deeply loyal to its own family. He behaves well with children too.

Country of Origin: Belgium

Training Notes: These tiny dogs are also known for maturing slowly. Some are four or five years old before they start acting like adults. Training is especially important for this stubborn breed. If an owner doesn't take the lead, the Schipperke surely will. The Schipperke is smart, though, so training isn't too difficult.

Care Notes: This active breed needs plenty of exercise. It does best when he has a fenced garden so it can run around and play often. Although Schipperkes shed, they usually only require weekly brushing and bathing.

Shar Pei

FUN FACT

The Shar Pei has a blue-black tongue that is most noticeable at the back of its mouth.

Appearance:
Height: 46 to 51 centimetres (18 to 20 inches)
Weight: 18 to 25 kilograms (40 to 55 pounds)

The Shar Pei is unique in appearance. Covered with wrinkles, a Shar Pei looks like it has too much skin for its body. The name *Shar Pei* actually means "sand skin". The breed's short, rough coat reminds many people of sand.

Personality: The Shar Pei is a devoted companion and an excellent watchdog. The breed can get along with other animals, as long as they are raised together.

Breed Background: These brave animals were developed as palace guards for Chinese royalty.

Country of Origin: China

Training Notes: Socialization is important for a Shar Pei because of its stubbornness. The instinct to guard runs deep in these dogs, so they need to be trained at an early age. Without firm handling, the Shar Pei will challenge its owner's authority.

Care Notes: The Shar Pei needs a lot of exercise. However, this breed is sensitive to heat. Similar to the Bulldog, a Shar Pei needs its wrinkles cleaned often.

Shih Tzu

FUN FACT

The name *Shih Tzu* means "lion" in Chinese.

Appearance:

Height: 25 to 28 centimetres (10 to 11 inches)
Weight: 4 to 7 kilograms (9 to 16 pounds)

The Shih Tzu (*SHEED-zoo*) has a sweet face that many owners say looks like a flower. Their long facial hair grows in every direction. Many owners keep a Shih Tzu's fur out of its face with a barrette or bow.

Their long double coats come in several colours. Shih Tzu may be all black, black and white, grey and white, or red and white. It can be hard to see this breed's legs beneath all its hair. When it walks briskly, a Shih Tzu almost looks seems to be floating.

Personality: This breed is one of the friendliest Utility group members. Bred to be pets, these dogs love people of all ages. Families with young children must teach children to be gentle with these small animals. Shih Tzu will usually get along well with other dogs and also cats.

Breed Background: The Shih Tzu was developed by crossing the Pekingese with the Lhasa Apso. Owned by nobility, these early dogs slept at the foot of their owners' beds. The dogs' job was to keep their owners' feet warm at night.

Country of Origin: China

Training Notes: Training Shih Tzu to follow basic commands is an easy task. House-training this breed may be challenging, however. Owners can improve their pet's chance of success by maintaining a strict schedule. Shih Tzu respond well to praise and rewards.

Care Notes: Shih Tzu have short muzzles that cause them to overheat quickly. During hot weather it is best to keep these dogs indoors with air conditioning. The Shih Tzu's long hair needs to be brushed at least once per week to prevent tangles. Daily walks and indoor playtime will usually meet their exercise needs.

FUN FACT

The name ***Shih Tzu*** is both singular and plural. Whether you have one dog or more, you have Shih Tzu.

Tibetan Spaniel

FUN FACT

Tibetan Spaniels get along with other dogs, and even cats, extremely well. This easy-going breed does well in a multi-pet household.

Appearance:
Height: 25 to 28 centimetres (10 to 11 inches)
Weight: 4 to 7 kilograms (9 to 15 pounds)

The Tibetan Spaniel is a small dog that looks like a little lion. The breed's silky double coat is smooth on its face and the front of its legs. The coat can be any colour or mix of colours. A Tibetan Spaniel has a plumed tail that curls over its back.

Personality: Tibetan Spaniels are extremely affectionate animals. They are sensitive to their owners' feelings. When people are sad or upset, this breed is right there to comfort them. Tibetan Spaniels love being included in family activities and thrive when owners giv[illegible]lenty of attention.

Country of Origi[illegible]

Training Notes: Tib[illegible] be stubborn at tim[illegible] easily. To help this bree[illegible] reliable pet, owners sh[illegible] when the dog is a puppy.

Care Notes: The Tibetan Spanie[illegible] is easy to groom. A walk or two each day is enough to fulfil its exercise needs. These curious little dogs must be kept on leads in public because of their natural curiosity to explore.

Tibetan Terrier

FUN FACT

The Tibetan Terrier's nickname is the "Holy Dog of Tibet".

Appearance:

Height: 36 to 41 centimetres (14 to 16 inches)
Weight: 9 to 11 kilograms (20 to 24 pounds)

The Tibetan Terrier has long, fine hair that may be straight or wavy. The double coat comes in a variety of colours and combinations. White, gold and silver are among the most popular.

Personality: This adaptive breed enjoys spending time indoors and out. While they don't need lots of exercise, they are more than happy to join in any activity. They just want to spend time with their favourite human family members. It is more than happy to be a [illegible]rd dog, too.

[illegible]**nd:** This breed [illegible]betan monks [illegible]

[illegible]**a:** Tibet

[illegible]**:** The Tibetan Terrier [illegible]o train. However, this dog gets [illegible]ily. Owners who use plenty of p[illegible]e and food rewards usually see the best results.

Care Notes: Tibetan Terriers need a large amount of grooming. As they grow into adults, their coats also grow. A dog needs daily brushing during this period to prevent tangles. A fully-grown Tibetan Terrier needs to be brushed about three times per week.

Intelligent companions

The Kennel Club's Working group is made up of 26 dog breeds. These dogs were developed to perform a variety of jobs. In the past they may have guarded castles or fought alongside their owners in historic battles. Some of these dogs still work as police or military dogs, sheep herders or sled dogs. A few breeds have even been known to perform more than one of these important jobs.

Many members of the working group are also popular as pets. These medium to large canines offer their human families love, companionship and often a certain amount of protection as well. One of the most common traits of this group is intense loyalty to the people they love most. Working dogs often crave a purpose. Outdoor pastimes, obedience training and organised activities can help fulfil this need in pets. Although these dogs share a lot of traits, each working dog breed has something unique to offer. Get ready for a close look at each one!

FUN FACT

The Kennel Club established the Young Kennel Club in 1985. This group helps young dog lovers between the ages of 6 and 24 to learn new skills, build confidence and make new friends.

Alaskan Malamute

FUN FACT

The Alaskan Malamute doesn't bark much. But it is vocal and will "talk" to its human family.

FAMOUS DOGS

Alaskan Malamutes appear in the films *Eight Below* and *Snow Dogs*.

Appearance:

Height: 58 to 64 centimetres (23 to 25 inches)
Weight: 34 to 39 kilograms (75 to 85 pounds)

Alaskan Malamutes have double coats that keep them warm in cold climates. Their coats have two layers, a coarse outer guard coat and a woolly undercoat. Their coats can be black, red or silver, but their faces are always white. Their plumed tails are held over their backs.

Personality: Alaskan Malamutes are extremely loyal and intelligent. They have a strong desire to hunt and capture prey, which makes them a poor match for homes with cats or other small animals. They are intensely loyal to their human families.

Breed Background: The name comes from Mahlemuts, an Alaskan tribe that raised these beautiful dogs. The Malamute is a Nordic-type dog which moved into the northern Polar regions when people began to occupy the land. The Mahlemut tribes were a hard-working and skilled Inuit (Eskimo) race who loved and cared for their dogs. Alaskan Malamutes are commonly used as sled dogs. Their powerful bodies make them perfect for this job.

Country of Origin: United States

Training Notes: Alaskan Malamutes are smart and highly trainable. House-training can be a challenge with this breed, however. Without firm leadership, these dogs can be **destructive**.

Care Notes: Alaskan Malamutes need a lot of exercise. But be careful not to over-exercise them in warm weather because they may overheat.

Even though a Malamute's hair resists dirt, its coat still needs regular brushing. This breed sheds very heavily.

FUN FACT

The Alaskan Malamute is descended from the Arctic wolf.

FUN FACT

An ideal Bernese Mountain Dog has a pattern on its chest that dog enthusiasts call a Swiss cross.

Bernese Mountain Dog

Appearance:
Height: 58 to 71 centimetres (23 to 28 inches)
Weight: 32 to 52 kilograms (70 to 115 pounds)

The Bernese Mountain Dog's coat is black, brown-red and white. While other Swiss mountain dogs share these colours, the Bernese is different. It is the only type with long, silky fur.

Personality: This breed has a pleasant temperament. Many Bernese Mountain Dogs love people, including children. Socialization is important, especially with other animals.

Country of Origin: Switzerland

Training Notes: Bernese Mountain Dogs are intelligent, but they can be slow learners. Positive training is key with this breed. Members of this breed can develop behaviour problems, such as excessive barking, chewing or digging if they spend too much time alone.

Care Notes: This breed loves outdoor activities, such as hiking. When properly exercised, Bernese Mountain Dogs won't misbehave as often. These dogs also need weekly grooming, including brushing.

Bouvier Des Flandres

FUN FACT

Bouvier Des Flandres worked as military dogs in World War I and World War II.

Appearance:

Height: 58 to 94 centimetres (23 to 37 inches)
Weight: 27 to 41 kilograms (60 to 90 pounds)

The Bouvier Des Flandres has a thick coat, and he comes in fawn, salt and pepper and brindle, which is brown with streaks. The fur covers the dog's face, forming its famous moustache and beard.

Personality: Bouviers are extremely dedicated animals. They make loyal pets, but they should be supervised around children and other animals. It is a quiet dog.

Breed Background: Belgian monks developed the Bouvier des Flandres breed. The word *bouvier* means "cattle herder" in French. These dogs are still used today to herd and protect cattle in Belgium and France.

Country of Origin: Belgium

Training Notes: These dogs are smart but independent. Bouviers need lots of training with positive reinforcement, such as praise and treats. Training should also be consistent from puppyhood to adulthood. Early socialization will also help a Bouvier adjust to meeting strangers.

Care Notes: These large, energetic dogs need plenty of room to run around. It is happy to live in the country or a city, and in a small home or large home. Bouviers also need to be brushed often to keep mats from forming.

FUN FACT

The Boxer was one of the first breeds used for police training in Germany.

Boxer

Appearance:
Height: 53 to 64 centimetres (21 to 25 inches)
Weight: 25 to 32 kilograms (55 to 70 pounds)

Boxer have short, shiny coats that are either brindle or fawn coloured. The breed has an athletic build and an alert expression. Boxers are compact and powerful. They are also known for their energy and extrovert personality.

Personality: Despite their sad look, these dogs are anything but gloomy. They often leap with excitement when they are happy. Boxers need to spend time with their human family members. They get along well with children too. They are high-spirited, playful and happy dogs. Boxers can be excellent watchdogs.

Breed Background: The Boxer was developed in Germany in the 1800s. The Boxer's ancestors were two German mastiff breeds, the Bullenbeiszer and the Barenbeiszer. Early Boxers were used for dog fighting and bull baiting, but those sports have since been outlawed. Boxers were also used as cattle dogs to round up livestock.

Country of Origin: Germany

Training Notes: When properly trained, Boxers are great at competitive obedience. Early training is important to keep their enthusiasm under control. This smart breed can be stubborn when it comes to training. The trick is making it fun. Dogs left alone too often can develop poor temperaments and behaviour problems.

Care Notes: Boxers need occasional grooming, including bathing. It is important to bathe a Boxer only when necessary, because it removes the natural oils from the skin.

Boxers need a lot of exercise. Boxers living in colder climates need to wear coats while outside. Their short hair cannot keep them warm enough.

FUN FACT

Some of the Boxer's many talents include guarding, military work, police work, search-and-rescue work, competitive obedience and performing tricks.

FUN FACT

Bullmastiffs were originally bred in England to guard large game against poachers.

Bullmastiff

Appearance:
Height: 61 to 69 centimetres (24 to 27 inches)
Weight: 45 to 59 kilograms (100 to 130 pounds)

Everything about the Bullmastiff is huge. From its square head to its massive body, this breed's size is its most remarkable feature. Its coat is short and smooth, and it can be any shade of brindle, fawn or red.

Personality: Bullmastiff owners often call their dogs "gentle giants". The breed isn't so easy-going with intruders, however. It is known as one of the bravest guard dogs.

Country of Origin: United Kingdom

Training Notes: Bullmastiffs can learn commands, but they don't always want to obey them. They need owners who are willing to train them continuously.

Care Notes: Owners need to keep a towel handy. These large dogs can produce a large amount of drool. Regular brushing will keep a Bullmastiff's coat in good condition.

Canadian Eskimo Dog

Appearance:
Height: 68 to 73 centimetres (27 to 29 inches)
Weight: 30 to 40 kilograms (66 to 88 pounds)

The Canadian Eskimo Dog looks a lot like a Siberian Husky. He has a thick double coat. It can be of any colour variety. The Canadian Eskimo dog is built for long-distance work.

Personality: The Canadian Eskimo Dog makes a great family pet because of its loyalty. It is alert and is sometimes known to howl loudly.

Breed Background: In the 1920s there were more than 20,000 Canadian Eskimo Dogs in Canada used as sled dogs. With the increasing popularity of snowmobiles, these sled dogs were replaced, and their numbers dropped down to about 200.

Country of Origin: Canada

Training Notes: Training a Canadian Eskimo Dog requires great patience. If an owner is not a firm "pack leader", the dog may become destructive. Consistent training, both mentally and physically, can help with this behavioural problem.

Care Notes: Canadian Eskimo Dogs need a fair amount of daily exercise. However, they should not be worked in hot weather. These dogs are heavy shedders twice per year. They should be brushed and bathed regularly.

FUN FACT

In some locations in Canada, this breed is called the Canadian Inuit Dog.

Dobermann

FUN FACT

In German the word *pinscher* refers to a dog's habit of jumping on and biting its prey.

Appearance:

Height: 61 to 71 centimetres (24 to 28 inches)
Weight: 29 to 41 kilograms (65 to 90 pounds)

The Dobermann has a sleek, muscular body. He usually has black and tan fur. Some Dobermanns can be brown, blue or fawn with rust-red markings.

Personality: The Dobermann is active, intelligent and loyal. It can also be described as fearless. It is a skilled tracker and used for police work.

Breed Background: German tax collector Louis Dobermann developed this breed in the late 1860s. He needed a dog that would protect him and encourage slow payers to pay their taxes.

Country of Origin: Germany

Training Notes: The Dobermann is one of the smartest dog breeds. It can learn almost any command. This breed needs a devoted and experienced owner, however. If Dobermanns aren't trained well, they can challenge their owners for control.

Care Notes: Dobermanns require only occasional bathing and brushing. These short-coated dogs do not do well in the cold. When spending time outside in cold weather, they need coats.

Dogue de Bordeaux

Appearance:
Height: 58 to 69 centimetres (23 to 27 inches)
Weight: 45 to 68 kilograms (99 to 150 pounds)

The Dogue de Bordeaux has a short, fawn coat. A wrinkled face, a massive head and a stocky body are trademarks of this breed. Despite its size it is able to jump high.

Personality: This breed has a personality as big as its body. This breed may act aggressively towards other dogs. However, if owners put work into training a Dogue de Bordeaux, they will end up with a good-natured pet.

Country of Origin: France

Training Notes: A Dogue de Bordeaux will try to get its way. It is the owner's job to train this breed before that happens. Early socialization and firm training are important.

Care Notes: The Dogue de Bordeaux drools – a lot! Owners should have drool rags handy. Their short coat is easy to care for with regular brushing.

FUN FACT

The Dogue de Bordeaux is also known as the French Mastiff.

FAMOUS DOGS

The character Hooch from the film *Turner & Hooch* is a Dogue de Bordeaux. Three different dogs played the role.

Entlebucher Mountain Dog

FUN FACT

The Entlebucher Mountain Dog is rarely seen outside its native land of Switzerland.

Appearance:
Height: 48 to 51 centimetres (19 to 20 inches)
Weight: 25 to 30 kilograms (55 to 66 pounds)

Similar to other Swiss mountain dogs, the Entlebucher (*ENT-leh-boo-cuhr*) is tricoloured with a primarily black body with tan and white markings. The top coat is short and shiny.

Personality: Although it is the smallest of all the Swiss mountain dogs, the Entlebucher is still a loyal and trusted companion and family member. He may try to herd small children, so the Entlebucher behaves best with older children. He may be reserved with strangers.

Breed Background: This breed originates from the Entlebuch Valley in Switzerland between Lucerne and Berne. Today it is still used as a cattle herding dog in the mountains of Switzerland.

Country of Origin: Switzerland

Training Notes: The Entlebucher responds well to positive, firm training. This breed excels at canine sports, such as agility.

Care Notes: An Entlebucher is easy to care for. Its short coat should be brushed regularly to keep it looking its best. An Entlebucher has a lot of energy. For this reason it enjoys daily walks or jogs.

Giant Schnauzer

Appearance:
Height: 58 to 71 centimetres (23 to 28 inches)
Weight: 29 to 41 kilograms (65 to 90 pounds)

The Giant Schnauzer is striking in every way. Its thick, wiry coat gives the dog a distinct look. This breed is usually black or a mixture of black and white, called salt and pepper.

Personality: These smart dogs demand lots of attention. Giant Schnauzers adore their human families. They are not the best choice for households with cats or other small animals because they love to chase prey.

Breed Background: Farmers around the Munich area in Germany used the Giant Schnauzer as a droving dog during the 1400s.

Country of Origin: Germany

Training Notes: Giant Schnauzers do well with training that is firm and consistent but not overly harsh.

Care Notes: Giant Schnauzers need a lot of daily exercise. Without it they can become destructive. Their coats also require time and effort because they tangle easily.

FUN FACT

The Giant Schnauzer is related to the Miniature Schnauzer and the Schnauzer. Each one is a separate breed, however.

Great Dane

FUN FACT

The word *Dane* means "from Denmark". But the breed's history has no known link to that country.

FAMOUS DOGS

The cartoon character Scooby-Doo is a Great Dane.

Appearance:
Height: 71 to 89 centimetres (28 to 35 inches)
Weight: 50 to 82 kilograms (110 to 180 pounds)

Great Danes are giant, powerful dogs. They have square bodies, long heads and dark eyes. Their ears are medium-sized and either stand **erect** or hang down the side of the head.

Great Danes come in a wide range of colours, including black, fawn and white with black spots. The spotted pattern is called harlequin.

Personality: Despite their large size, Great Danes are gentle dogs. They are especially affectionate with their human family members. These dogs love people. Great Danes are excellent watchdogs.

Breed Background: The Great Dane is a very old dog breed. The earliest writings about Great Danes were in Chinese literature in 1121 BC. Dogs that looked like Great Danes appeared on Greek money dating back to 36 BC. Used as a hunting dog for wild boar, the Great Dane has also been the national dog of Germany since 1876.

Country of Origin: Germany

Training Notes: Great Danes are willing students when it comes to training. Training should begin early in a Great Dane's life. Great Danes do not stay little for long. They should be taught not to lean on or jump on people. To avoid behavioural problems, such as aggression, early socialization should be a priority in a Great Dane's training.

Care Notes: The short, smooth coat of a Great Dane is easy to groom. Great Danes require only occasional bathing and brushing. Owners must feed this gigantic animal lots of food.

Great Danes need plenty of exercise, so a long, daily walk is recommended. But beware! Because this breed is strong, a Great Dane that pulls when walking on a lead may end up taking its owner for a walk instead.

FUN FACT

The litters of Great Danes tend to be larger than other dog breeds. One Great Dane reportedly produced a litter of 19 puppies!

FUN FACT

Greenland Dogs are extremely rare. Most Greenland owners either imported their pet from Greenland or took one home after a visit there.

Greenland Dog

Appearance:
Height: 56 to 64 centimetres (22 to 25 inches)
Weight: 30 to 32 kilograms (66 to 70 pounds)

The Greenland Dog has a thick double coat. Its dense coat is meant to withstand temperatures as cold as –45 to –55 degrees Celsius (–50 to –65 degrees Fahrenheit). He comes in many colours variations too.

Personality: Although it is independent, the Greenland Dog will bond with its human family members. It does not like to sit around the house all day. This breed thrives on some kind of activity.

Breed Background: The ancestry of this dog can be traced back to regions near Siberia more than 12,000 years ago.

Country of Origin: Greenland

Training Notes: Because these dogs are independent, training Greenlands can be difficult. Firm, patient leadership works best with this breed.

Care Notes: This dog should be brushed regularly, as it is a shedder. The Greenland Dog does best with an active owner, as it needs a lot of regular exercise.

Hovawart

FUN FACT

The Hovawart has a distinct, deep-throated bark that will protect against intruders.

Appearance:

Height: 56 to 64 centimetres (22 to 25 inches)
Weight: 30 to 32 kilograms (66 to 70 pounds)

The Hovawart has medium-length fur that can either be straight or slightly wavy. The hair is shorter on its head and the front of its legs. A Hovawart is either black, blond or black and gold.

Personality: The Hovawart makes a great family pet as long as he gets its exercise. It is a loyal family dog and generally will not wander far away. It is also a great watchdog.

Breed Background: Records of this dog date back as far as the 1200s. For many centuries, this breed was known as a guard dog, mainly on farmyards.

Country of Origin: Germany

Training Notes: Early socialization is important for this breed. Stimulation is also important for Hovawarts. Without it, behavioural problems such as biting can become an issue.

Care Notes: The Hovawart's hair is easy to care for. Its hair should be brushed and bathed occasionally. An owner should take special care of areas prone to tangling. The Hovawart should be taken on a daily walk, jog or run. It will also appreciate the chance to run and play off the lead.

Leonberger

FUN FACT

Leonbergers have been owned by many royal families, including Napoleon II of France, the Prince of Wales and Empress Elizabeth of Austria.

Appearance:
Height: 74 to 80 centimetres (29 to 31 inches)
Weight: 59 to 77 kilograms (130 to 170 pounds)

The Leonberger ia a large, muscular working dog. Its double coat can be lion gold, red, red-brown, sandy or any combination of these colours.

Personality: The Leonberger is a loving dog with a sweet expression. It has a lot of love and loyalty for its human family.

Breed Background: Established in the 1840s in Leonberg, Germany, this dog was bred to closely resemble a lion. By the end of World War II, as few as eight Leonbergers existed. It took more than 25 years for the breed to be firmly re-established. The Leonberger has been successful for guarding livestock, search-and-rescue missions and tracking.

Country of Origin: Germany

Training Notes: The Leonberger is eager to please its owners. However, it does not respond well to harsh training, therefore calm and consistent methods work best.

Care Notes: Weekly brushing is needed, but the Leonberger should only be bathed when necessary. It does not require a great deal of exercise. However, it should be taken on a daily walk. It loves to swim too.

Mastiff

FUN FACT

Drawings of Mastiffs on Egyptian monuments date back to 3000 BC.

Appearance:
Height: 69 to 91 centimetres (27 to 36 inches)
Weight: 79 to 86 kilograms (175 to 190 pounds)

The Mastiff is an extra-large dog with a short double coat. The fur can be one of several colours, including fawn or orange-yellow, which is called apricot.

Personality: These massive animals have surprisingly sweet temperaments. The Mastiff is affectionate.The biggest battle owners usually face is getting these large dogs off the sofa.

Country of Origin:
United Kingdom

Training Notes: Training is important because of the breed's size. Starting early is smart because Mastiffs can be stubborn learners. Socialization is important to prevent Mastiffs from being wary of strangers.

Care Notes: A Mastiff's short coat makes grooming an easy task. This large dog only needs an occasional bath and brushing. Although these dogs are lazy, regular exercise is important.

Neapolitan Mastiff

FUN FACT

Julius Caesar owned Neapolitan Mastiffs during the 100s BC.

Appearance:
Height: 61 to 79 centimetres (24 to 31 inches)
Weight: 50 to 68 kilograms (110 to 150 pounds)

The Neapolitan Mastiff looks similar to the Mastiff. The biggest difference is size. The Neapolitan is slightly smaller.

Personality: This breed is strong in both body and will. Neapolitans have been described as stubborn, lazy and independent. Many members of the breed also have a strong dislike for other dogs.

Country of Origin: Italy

Training Notes: The Neapolitan Mastiff needs firm guidance with training. Early socialization is necessary for this breed to become a well-mannered pet.

Care Notes: Neapolitan Mastiffs bond closely with their human families. They can suffer from **separation anxiety** if left alone too much. A Neapolitan also needs to be brushed every other week to keep its coat looking its best.

Newfoundland

Appearance:

Height: 64 to 74 centimetres (25 to 29 inches)
Weight: 45 to 68 kilograms (100 to 150 pounds)

The Newfoundland has a heavy double coat. The fur, which lies close to the body, naturally resists water. He comes in several colours, including black, brown and white.

Personality: It is hard to say what Newfoundlands love more – the water or children. For this reason the breed's ideal day is spent with its human family at the lake.

Breed Background: Some people believe the Newfoundland is a cross between a Tibetan Mastiff and a Labrador. Long ago in the 1700s, these dogs worked with fishermen, pulling nets filled with their catches.

Country of Origin: Canada

Training Notes: The Newfoundland needs training due to its large size. Newfoundlands respond well to gentle, positive training and early socialization.

Care Notes: The breed's only demanding trait is its need for grooming. All that fur requires combing twice per week. This gentle giant should also be taken on a daily walk.

FUN FACT

Newfoundlands have large lungs, which makes them good at long-distance swimming.

FAMOUS DOGS

Nana from *Peter Pan* is a Newfoundland.

Portuguese Water Dog

Appearance:
Height: 43 to 58 centimetres (17 to 23 inches)
Weight: 16 to 27 kilograms (35 to 60 pounds)

Many people mistake curly-coated Portuguese Water Dogs for Poodles. The breed comes in two coat types. Short-coated Porties have tight, dense curls. The longer coat variety is made up of loose waves.

Personality: This dog's pleasant temperament makes it a popular pet. These dogs can be shy with strangers, but they love their human families. It is friendly but self-willed.

Breed Background: Portuguese Water Dogs have a long history of working in the water. The breed once carried messages between ships for Spanish sailors.

Country of Origin: Portugal

Training Notes: The breed is intelligent and learns commands easily. Porties respond well to positive training.

Care Notes: The Portuguese Water Dog's coat is considered hypoallergenic. Its coat should be brushed weekly. These dogs are also very athletic and need a lot of exercise.

▲

FAMOUS DOGS

Two Portuguese Water Dogs have made their way to the White House in the US. The Obama family welcomed Bo (left) in 2009. Sunny (right) joined him in 2013.

FUN FACT

In its native land, it is called the *Cão de Água*, which means "dog of water".

Rottweiler

Appearance:

Height: 56 to 69 centimetres (22 to 27 inches)
Weight: 36 to 61 kilograms (80 to 135 pounds)

The Rottweiler looks like the Dobermann's big brother. Their coats are the same black and tan pattern. But the Rottie is much heavier and more powerful.

Personality: This breed can be a loving, relaxed dog with its human family. Rotties are naturally protective.

Breed Background: During the Middle Ages, Rottweilers were used as herders, guard dogs, messenger dogs and for police work.

Country of Origin: Germany

Training Notes: Training must begin during puppyhood. Left untrained, a Rottweiler is likely to become aggressive. These smart dogs learn quickly and easily. Still, a Rottie must understand who the leader is at all times. Early obedience training is recommended.

Care Notes: Rottweilers need lots of activity and stimulation. Hiking, swimming, or organised activities, such as agility, can fulfil this need. Their coat should be brushed every other week.

FUN FACT

The Rottweiler is a descendent of ancient Roman drover dogs. These dogs helped move livestock, such as cattle, long distances.

Saint Bernard

FUN FACT

A Saint Bernard can smell a person buried under 6 metres (20 feet) of snow.

FAMOUS DOGS

Beethoven from the film and cartoon series of the same name is a Saint Bernard.

Appearance:
Height: 64 to 69 centimetres (25 to 27 inches)
Weight: 54 to 91 kilograms (120 to 200 pounds)

Saint Bernards come in two coat types – short and long. Short-haired dogs have a surprising amount of hair. The long-haired variety has even more. Both come in mixtures of red and white.

Personality: Saint Bernards can make excellent family companions. These dogs are loyal and loving. Despite their size, they are great with children.

Breed Background: The Saint Bernard is known throughout the world for its bravery. This breed has a heroic history of rescuing more than 2,000 people caught in **avalanches**.

Country of Origin: Switzerland

Training Notes: These dogs are smart and easily trainable. Because of their large size, Saint Bernards should begin training as puppies to learn not to jump on people or steal food from the table.

Care Notes: This huge pet needs encouragement to get enough exercise. A Saint Bernard also produces a large amount of drool, so drool rags are a must-have with this dog.

Siberian Husky

Appearance:
Height: 51 to 61 centimetres (20 to 24 inches)
Weight: 16 to 27 kilograms (35 to 60 pounds)

At first glance Siberian Huskies look a lot like Alaskan Malamutes. Both breeds are common choices for sled dogs. But the Siberian Husky shares more physical traits with its ancestor, the wolf.

Personality: A Husky's temperament is not wild like a wolf's. Huskies adore people, including children. They also get along well with other dogs.

Country of Origin: Russia

Training Notes: Siberian Huskies are intelligent dogs. They respond well to positive training methods. House-training may be difficult for this breed as well.

Care Notes: Fenced gardens and leads are musts, as Huskies are known runners. Despite their high tolerance for cold weather, these dogs should not be kept outdoors all the time. Their thick coats should be brushed every other week.

FUN FACT

Some Siberian Huskies have one blue and one brown eye.

Other working breeds

German Pinscher ▶

Appearance:
Height: 41 to 48 centimetres (16 to 19 inches)
Weight: 11 to 16 kilograms (25 to 35 pounds)
Known for: hunting rats and later as guard dogs
Country of Origin: Germany

Greater Swiss Mountain Dog

Appearance:
Height: 60 to 72 centimetres (24 to 29 inches)
Weight: 59 to 61 kilograms (130 to 135 pounds)
Known for: driving cattle and pulling carts
Country of Origin: Switzerland

Russian Black Terrier ▼

Appearance:

Height: 64 to 74 centimetres (25 to 29 inches)

Weight: 36 to 65 kilograms (80 to 143 pounds)

Known for: working as military dogs

Country of Origin: Russia

Glossary

agility ability to move fast and easily

aggressive strong and forceful

aloof distant or not friendly

avalanche large mass of ice, snow or earth that suddenly moves down the side of a mountain

bait annoy or taunt

boisterous noisy, energetic and rowdy

bow bend in a curved line

breed standard list of ideal traits for a member of a specific dog breed, such as appearance and temperament

brindle brown, tawny colour of animal fur, with streaks of another colour

bristle one of the long, wiry hairs used to make brushes

dander skin flakes in an animal's fur or hair

descendant person or animal who comes from a particular group of ancestors

destructive causing lots of damage

earthdog trial test for small dogs to assess their hunting ability and instincts

erect standing upright

fawn light brown colour

feeble very weak

gait way of walking

heartworm tiny worm carried by mosquitoes that enters a dog's heart and slowly destroys it

hypoallergenic possessing a quality that reduces or eliminates allergic reactions

mascot person or animal that represents a sports team or organisation

mat thick, tangled mass of hair

muzzle animal's nose, mouth and jaws

obedience obeying rules and commands

obesity extremely overweight

persist keep on doing something in spite of obstacles or warnings

plume spread out in a shape resembling a feather

poacher person who hunts or fishes illegally

pointer type of dog breed used for hunting, flushing and retrieving game

purebred having ancestors of the same breed or kind of animal

quarry animal hunted as prey

rally dog sport based on obedience

ratter person, animal, or thing that catches rats

retrieve bring something back

ruff ring of long hair around a dog's neck

sable black or dark brown

saddle coloured marking on the back of an animal

separation anxiety distressful canine condition that occurs when a dog is away from its owner

setter one of several breeds of hunting dogs that are trained to stand stiffly and point the muzzle toward the scented game

socialize train a dog to get along with people and other dogs

stimulate encourage interest or activity in a person or animal

strip process of removing dead hair from an animal's fur by hand or with a stripping tool

temperament combination of an animal's behaviour and personality; the way an animal usually acts or responds to situations shows its temperament

texture the way something feels when you touch it

tolerance ability to put up with or endure something, such as pain or hardship

track follow someone or something; a technique in which dogs are trained to locate an object using its scent

tricolour having three colours

tuxedo suit for men to be worn on special occasions

unruly hard to control or discipline

vermin any of various small, common insects or animals that are harmful pests

weatherproof resistant to the effects of bad weather, especially rain

Index

Photo Credits:

Alamy: Moviestore Collection Ltd., 190 (bottom); Corbis: Asa Lindholm/Naturbild, 83 (top), Dorling Kindersley Ltd, 83 (b); Dreamstime: Chrispethick, cover; Newscom: Chris Brignell/Photoshot, 106 (b), Dorling Kindersley, 30 (b), 50 (b), 56 (b), 82 (b), 88 (b), 138 (b), 154 (b), Ron Sachs/CNP/Polaris, 198 (t), Yves Lanceau/NHPA/ Photoshot, 124 (t); Shutterstock: Aleksandra Dabrowa, 79 (t), Alena Kazlouskaya, 85, Alex White, 11 (t), Ammit Jack, 94-95, Andreas Gradin, 22 (b), 25 (b), 120, Andrey Burmakin, 169 (b), AnetaPics, 96 (t), 158, 178, Anna Tyurina, 100 (t), ANURAK PONGPATIMET, 144 (b), Antonio Guillem, 173, artcphotos, 20 (t), ARTSILENSE, 38 (b), 89 (b), B&T Media Group, Inc., 183, BarboraPeskova, 193 (t), Barna Tanko, 15 (t), Balazs Kovacs Images, 142 (t), belu gheorghe, 190 (t), Best dog photo, 72 (t), Bildagentur Zoonar GmbH, 68, 113 (t), 162 (t), BORTEL Pavel-Pavelmidi, 132 (t), Burry van den Brink, 12 (t), c.byatt-norman, 24 (t), Ca, 107 (t), callalloo, 114 (t), Capture Light, 46 (t), 73 (t), 98 (t), 102 (t), 111 (t), 115 (t), 125 (t), Christian Mueller, 157 (t), Csanad Kiss, 15 (b), 81 (b), CyberKat, 10 (t), cynoclub, 10 (b), 18 (b), 35, 63, 40 (b), 66 (t), 71 (b), 72 (b), 100 (b), 104 (b), 110 (b), 111 (b), 181 (t), Dennis Jacobsen, 130 (t), dien, 136 (t), 166 (b), Dioniya, 201 (t), Dmitry Kalinovsky, 96 (b), dogist, 167 (t), Dora Zett, 42 (b), 152 (t), Dorottya Mathe, 134 (b), DragoNika, 14 (t), 38 (t), 54, 61 (t), 42 (t), 140 (t), 186 (t), eAlisa, 114 (b), Elena Kutepova, 189 (t), Eric Isselee, backcover, 1 (right), 12 (b), 24 (b), 26 (b), 27 (b), 28 (b), 48 (b), 55, 60 (b), 61 (b), 66 (b), 67 (b), 69, 70 (b), 74 (b), 75 (b), 78 (b), 79 (b), 80 (b), 92, 101 (b), 102 (b), 113 (b), 115 (b), 116 (b), 117 (b), 127, 130 (b), 131 (b), 132 (b), 136 (b), 139 (b), 150 (b), 152 (b), 156 (b), 157 (b), 159, 160 (b), 162 (b), 165 (b), 170 (b), 175 (b), 179, 180 (b), 192 (b), 193 (b), 194 (b), 197 (b), 200 (b), 202, 203, Erik Lam, 7 (bottom left), 11 (b), 20 (b), 29 (b), 34 (b), 44 (b), 98 (b), 99 (b), 105 (b), 119 (b), 128 (b), 137 (b), 164 (b), 174 (b), 184 (b), 196 (b), evastudio, 145 (t), f8grapher, 126, 184 (t), Fedor Sellvanov, 200 (t), gbarinov, 43 (b), Goldika, 135 (t), Grisha Bruev, 45 (t), GroanGarbu, 81 (t), HelenaQueen, 91, holbox, 122-123, Iakov Filimonovlev, 16 (b), Idea Studio, 199 (t), Igor Marx, 7 (bottom right), 188 (b), Igor Norman, 36-37, IMANDRA, 174 (t), Irina oxilixo Danilova, 6, 23 (b), 47, Ivonne Wierink, 14 (b), JP Chretien, 70 (t), Jagodka, 21 (b), 31 (b), 45 (b), 46 (b), 49 (b), 52 (b), 87 (b), 97 (b), 133 (t), 143, 167 (b), 186 (b), 195 (b), 199 (b), Joakim Lloyd Raboff, 124 (b), Jody., 31 (t), Joy Prescott, 118 (t), Judy Kennamer, 139 (t), Juha Saastamoinen, 164 (t), Julia Remezova, 67 (t), 172 (b), juliazara, 8-9. Justin Black, 17 (t), Kachalkkina Veronika, 89 (t), Ksenia Raykova, 74 (t), LarsTuchel, 182 (t), Lee319, 71 (t), 87 (t), 168 (t), 170 (t), Lenkadan, 26 (t), 27 (t), 44 (t), 57 (t), 75 (t), 112 (t), 131 (t), 155 (t), lev radin, 99 (t), Liliya Kulianionak, 90, 150 (t), 155 (b), Linn Currie, 19 (t), 23 (t), Lipowski Milan, 107 (b), Lorenzo Patoia, 28 (t), magdanphoto, 73 (b), manfredxy, 175 (t), Marcel Jancovic, 82 (t), Marlonneke Willemsen, 109, Michal Ninger, 195 (t), michael d skelton, 146 (t), Mikkel Bigandt, backcover, 1 (middle), 32, 64-65, 134 (t), Mitrofanov Alexander, 166 (t), Nancy Bauer, 185 (t), Nata Sdobnikova, 121 (b), 201 (b), Natalia V Guseva, 97 (t), 116 (t), Nejron Photo, backcover, 1 (left), 33, Nikolai Tsvetkov, 76, 77, 119 (t), nicolasdecorte, 18 (t), O. Bellini, backcover, 140 (b), oksana2010, 142 (b), Oleg Znamenskiy, 161 (t), Orientgold, 16 (t), otsphoto, 21 (t), 194 (t), Pack-Shot, 154 (t), Pavel Shlykov, 188 (t), pavelmayorov, 171 (t), Pelevinia Ksinia, 59, Phil Date, 125 (b), Phil Stev, 22 (t), photocell, 105 (t), Quayside, 17 (b), rebeccaashworth, 30 (t), 172 (t), Richard Chaff, 117 (t), Rita Kochmarjova, 41 (t), 133 (b), Robin Heal, 192 (t), Robynrg, 62 (t), 118 (b), Roger costa morera, 176-177, Rowena, 60 (t), RTimages, 168 (t), saasemen, 49 (t), Sally Wallis, 53 (t), Sanne vd Berg Fotografie, 181 (b), Sbolotova, 86 (t), Scandphoto, 78 (t), Schubbel, 80 (t), Sergey Fatin, 156 (t), Sergey Lavrentev, 141 (b), 147 (b), SikorskiFotografie, 34 (t), siloto, 43 (t), steamroller_blues, 161 (b), SteffiMueller, 129 (t), Steve Lovegrove, 48 (t), Stieber, 128 (t), StockPhotosLV, 29 (t), Susan Schmitz, backcover, 86 (b), 93, 151, 153 (b), 198 (b), Svetlana Valoueva, 40 (t), 84, 101 (t), 104 (t), 138 (t), tankist276, 129 (b), Tatiana Katsai, 58, TatyanaPanova, 169 (t), 171 (b), teekaygee, 180 (t), terekhov Igor, 50 (t), The Dog Photographer, 148-149, Timolina, 145 (b), tsik, 52 (t), 147 (t), Utekhina Anna, 135 (b), V.Belov, 25 (t), Vera Zinkova, 160 (t), vgm, 137 (t), Vicente Barcelo Varona, 146 (b), violetblue, 112 (b), 121 (t), Vitaly Titov & Maria Sidelnikova, 187, Vivienstock, backcover, 5, 39 (b), 62 (b), 189 (b), 191, VKarlov, 108, 141 (t), 144 (t), 165 (t), 196 (t), volofin, 39 (t), Voltgroup, 185 (b), vtls, 110 (t), WilleeCole Photography, 19 (b), 57 (b), 153 (t), www.BillionPhoto, 41 (b), YAN WEN,197 (t); Superstock: Jean-Michel Labat/ardea.com/Pantheon, 53 (b), John Daniels/ardea.com/ Panth/Pantheon, 56 (t), Juniors/Juniors, 88 (t), Marka/Marka, 106 (t)

First published in 2017 by Curious Fox, an imprint of Capstone Global Library Limited, 264 Banbury Road, Oxford, OX2 7DY – Registered company number: 6695582
www.curious-fox.com

ISBN 978-1-78202-489-7
21 20 19 18 17
10 9 8 7 6 5 4 3 2

A CIP catalogue for this book is available from the British Library.

Previously published as seven library-bound editions:
ISBN: 978-1-4747-2082-3
ISBN: 978-1-4747-2083-0
ISBN: 978-1-4747-2084-7
ISBN: 978-1-4747-2085-4
ISBN: 978-1-4747-2086-1
ISBN: 978-1-4747-2087-8
ISBN: 978-1-4747-2088-5

Editorial Credits
Alesha Sullivan, editor; Terri Poburka and Tracy McCabe, designers; Kelly Garvin, media researcher; Katy LaVigne, production specialist

Printed and bound in China.